A RAINBOW OVER NORTHERN FOOTHILLS OF THE SIERRA MADRE OCCIDENTAL

BEAKED YUCCA IN A ROCK-BOUND ARROYO, CUATRO CIENEGAS BASIN

A SWEEP OF SAND DUNES, WESTERN CHIHUAHUAN DESERT

THE 980-FOOT BASASEACHIC FALLS, NORTH OF BARRANCA DEL COBRE

GARAMBULLO CACTUS IN A LAVA FIELD EAST OF SAN LUIS POTOSI

FORESTED VOLCANIC TERRAIN NORTH-WEST OF GUADALAJARA

SUMMER-BLOOMING ORANGE CALTROP IN THE CHIHUAHUAN GRASSLANDS

PEOPLES OF THE WILD
THE EPIC OF FLIGHT
THE SEAFARERS
WORLD WAR II
THE GOOD COOK
THE TIME-LIFE ENCYCLOPAEDIA
OF GARDENING
HUMAN BEHAVIOUR
THE GREAT CITIES
THE ART OF SEWING
THE OLD WEST
THE WORLD'S WILD PLACES
THE EMERGENCE OF MAN
LIFE LIBRARY OF PHOTOGRAPHY
THIS FABULOUS CENTURY
TIME-LIFE LIBRARY OF ART
FOODS OF THE WORLD
GREAT AGES OF MAN
LIFE SCIENCE LIBRARY
LIFE NATURE LIBRARY
YOUNG READERS LIBRARY
LIFE WORLD LIBRARY
THE TIME-LIFE BOOK OF BOATING
TECHNIQUES OF PHOTOGRAPHY
LIFE AT WAR
LIFE GOES TO THE MOVIES
BEST OF LIFE

MEXICO'S SIERRA MADRE

THE WORLD'S WILD PLACES/TIME-LIFE BOOKS/AMSTERDAM

BY DONALD DALE JACKSON AND PETER WOOD

AND THE EDITORS OF TIME-LIFE BOOKS

WITH PHOTOGRAPHS BY DAN BUDNIK

THE WORLD'S WILD PLACES

EDITOR: Robert Morton
Editorial Staff for *Mexico's Sierra Madre:*
Text Editor: Marion Buhagiar
Picture Editor: Jane D. Scholl
Designer: Charles Mikolaycak
Staff Writer: Carol Clingan
Chief Researcher: Martha T. Goolrick
Researchers: Peggy Bushong, Muriel Clarke,
Lea G. Gordon, Beatrice Hsia, Janice Pikey,
Editha Yango
Design Assistant: Vincent Lewis
Picture Co-ordinator: Joan T. Lynch
Copy Co-ordinator: Susan Tribich

Revisions Staff:
SENIOR EDITOR: Rosalind Stubenberg
Chief Researcher: Barbara Levitt
Text Editor: Sarah Brash
Researcher: Martha Reichard George
Copy Co-ordinator: Cynthia Kleinfeld
Art Assistant: Jeanne Potter
Editorial Assistants: Mary Kosak, Linda Yates

ISBN 7054 0169 3

TIME-LIFE is a trademark of Time Incorporated U.S.A.

Published by Time-Life Books B.V.
Ottho Heldringstraat 5, 1066 AZ Amsterdam.

Editors' Note: Because the Sierra Madre is a great, sprawling region covering some 580,000 square miles of mountains and high deserts, this book has been written by two authors who visited the area separately. The first two chapters were written by Donald Dale Jackson; the last three and the Nature Walk were written by Peter Wood.

The Authors: Donald Dale Jackson spent two months in Texas and Mexico hiking, camping and caving to gather material for *Mexico's Sierra Madre.* Formerly with *Life,* he has written *Aeronauts* and *Flying the Mail* for Time-Life Books series The Epic of Flight. Jackson has written articles on sports and the outdoors, as well as books on American judges and the California gold rush.

Peter Wood climbed mountains and probed deserts to gather research for this book. An enthusiastic skin-diver and small-boat sailor, he wrote *Caribbean Isles* in this series, as well as *The Spanish Main,* a volume in the Time-Life Books series The Seafarers. Wood has also produced many magazine articles and a book on squash, a sport in which he has been a nationally ranked player in the United States of America.

The Photographer: Dan Budnik, a native of New York's Long Island, switched from painting to photography in the early 1950s; his first picture essay appeared in *Life en Español* in 1956. Since then his work has been widely published and exhibited; ecology is a favourite subject. His photographs are featured in five other books in The World's Wild Places series, as well as in a book about Rome in Time-Life Books series, The Great Cities.

The Cover: Laid bare by erosion, the volcanic ribs of Mexico's great western range—the Sierra Madre Occidental—lie exposed in a 4,000-foot-deep cleft known as the Barranca del Cobre, or Copper Canyon. Abysses such as this one, whose flanks are gouged by small arroyos, are a striking characteristic of the Occidental. In the Sierra Madre Oriental to the east, erosion has carved lesser canyons from the limestone bedrock, and ground water has eaten out labyrinthine caves and pits more than 1,400 feet deep.

Contents

1/ Across the Rio Grande 20

Gateway to the Sierra Madre 36

2/ The Dark Heart of the Cordillera 52

A Nature Walk in Cuatro Ciénegas Basin 68

3/ Where the Birds Are 84

A Glorious Botanical Confusion 104

4/ An Ocean of Mountains 118

Changing Face of the Desert 136

5/ The Barranca Country 148

Austere Beauty of a Far Place 166

Bibliography 180

Acknowledgements and Credits 181

Index 182

The Rough Embrace of the Sierra Madre

From the Big Bend country of Texas and the border of Arizona, the two great arms of Mexico's Sierra Madre —the Oriental on the east and the Occidental to the west—stretch down to Guadalajara and Ciudad de México (Mexico City) some 800 miles. Though pocketed with settlements, the two rough chains and the high desert basin between them encompass wilderness areas of extraordinary variety and grandeur. They include the unique gypsum dunes in the oasis at Cuatro Ciénegas (pages 68-82) and the cloud forest on the moist, Gulf-facing slopes of the Oriental south of Ciudad Victoria (pages 104-116), as well as the plunging barrancas that render some sections of the western range almost impassable.

On the map at left, national parks and forests, Indian reservations and public lands are indicated by red outlines; points of specific scenic interest, such as caves, are marked with black squares; mountain peaks are identified with black triangles. The notorious Comanche trail once used by Indians to raid in Mexico is shown as a dotted line. Desert areas are indicated with red dots and sand dunes are marked with patterned red dots.

1/ Across the Río Grande

*Colour was as extraordinary as form there—black,
yellow, vermilion, white, brown, buff, all
altered by distance and heat, all given mystery
by every variation of light.* PAUL HORGAN/ GREAT RIVER

I stood on a cactus-covered hill in the south-east corner of Big Bend
National Park, Texas, and stared across the slender brown band of the
Río Grande at Mexico. I could see a small farmhouse on the narrow
floodplain and the treeless, white-walled village of Boquillas perhaps
three miles down river. Between the two was a rocky trail that climbed
a hill behind the farm, then skirted the edge of a cliff. The trail was no
more than 100 yards from where I stood. A red-tailed hawk flew a
holding pattern high above the cliff.

In a few minutes two boys on a single burro came ambling up the
trail, talking animatedly. I watched their slow progress until they vanished from sight. Then a man in a broad-brimmed hat and a white shirt
came up the trail on foot with a boy. The boy would walk for a time,
fall behind, then run at top speed until he caught up with the man, chattering all the while. I guessed that they were a farmer and son on their
way to the village. I waited until the man saw me watching him and,
feeling slightly foolish, I waved. He stopped for a few seconds, stared
at me, then continued on without returning my wave.

Only a few hundred yards behind me on the American side, beyond a
hilltop fringed with spindly ocotillo shrubs, was an elaborate caravan
site—paved in asphalt, carefully marked and sectioned off. It was
equipped with rest rooms, water taps and small grills. Smoke curled
up from the stove vents of a dozen large motor caravans. Along the

path I had taken up the hill there had been neatly printed signs that identified and described various plants.

It occurred to me, as I watched the Mexican's retreating back, that he and the caravan tourists could have changed places in 15 minutes, but each would have been bewildered in the other's world. The Río Grande at this point and at this time of year—December, the beginning of the dry season—was no more than a shallow stream, only about 25 yards across and maybe two and a half feet deep. But the cultural chasm separating the two societies on either side of the border was immense.

Yet the river is just an arbitrary boundary: a political rather than a physical border. Along this section, Río Grande seems very much a misnomer; there is nothing *grande* about it. It is simply a desert stream, easily forded. The landscape is essentially the same on each side of it. Both sides belong to the same biotic province; that is, an area with plant and animal communities recognizably different from those of adjacent areas.

Biologists call this province the Chihuahuan Desert region. It is a vast stretch of land, reaching from the sagebrush country of the Southwestern United States to deep inside Mexico. Big Bend National Park is a part of the Chihuahuan Desert region, and so are the northern extremities of the two great Mexican mountain ranges that were the ultimate destination on this journey of exploration: the Sierra Madre Oriental (Eastern) and the Sierra Madre Occidental (Western).

To most *norteamericanos*, any mention of the Sierra Madre conjures up the treasure of gold that attracted Humphrey Bogart and his greedy companions in a celebrated Hollywood film. My motive for going to the Sierra Madre was considerably less complicated: I simply wanted to see a sprawling wilderness that the casual visitor never reaches. There are no tourist caravans in the heart of the Sierra Madre, no luxurious hotels and very little English spoken. These reclusive mountains offer no easy welcome. On the other hand, there is much to reward the persistent intruder, including some of the most spectacular land forms in the Western Hemisphere.

The Occidental and Oriental ranges sweep southwards in Majestic parallel ramparts, jostling the clouds at altitudes of up to 12,000 feet for 775 miles in the west and 810 miles in the east. But it is not their snowy heights, nor their dramatic sweep, nor their peaks, strangely sculpted by erosion, that create the impression of grandiose scale. It is their breadth. Both the Occidental and the Oriental are so broad—each more than 100 miles across—that from the air they appear as endless wavy ranks fading into and beyond the horizon. Looking west through a pass in the Oriental, the traveller can see six or seven distinct ridge lines before the contours are lost to haze.

Close up, the Occidental and the Oriental differ markedly. The Occidental, born of volcanic upheaval, is more rugged, more austere. The Oriental, composed largely of limestone laid down by an ancient sea that once covered the region, is lusher and slightly more gentle. The differing origins of the ranges reveal themselves in some extraordinary interior features. The Occidental has stupendous waterfalls, one of which, Basaseáchic, plunges almost 1,000 feet. The Occidental also contains complex, steep-sided canyons called barrancas, some of which plunge to depths that rival the Grand Canyon of the Colorado.

The limestone of the Oriental is pocked with colossal, multichambered caves and, at various places where cave ceilings have collapsed, with the vertical open pits called *sótanos*. The word *sótano* is Spanish for basement, but the imagery is inadequate. The pits are of dizzying depths; some penetrate as far as 1,400 feet into the earth, deep enough to accommodate the Empire State Building.

The Oriental and the Occidental share one fascinating feature. Because of their sheer length, hundreds upon hundreds of miles through varying latitudes and temperatures, both ranges undergo radical transformations as they sweep south. In the north they are desert regions, sandy and dry, dotted with creosote bush and mesquite, yucca and ocotillo and a host of other plants that have made their peace with aridity. Farther south, where the ranges increase in altitude, their peaks and high draws are home to trees and wild flowers of the temperate zones. The ranges enter still another environment as they cross the Tropic of Cancer: a humid, thickly carpeted jungle of tropical plants and the forms of animal life sustained by heavy rainfall.

Untamed and unyielding, Sierra Madre country is still an arena of human struggle. Hatchet-wielding woodcutters work the high pine forests; farmers cultivate isolated plots of coffee and other crops a day's climb from the nearest village. A simple fact of topography forces the agricultural Mexican up the mountainsides: only a third of Mexico's land is relatively level, and much of that is arid. The result, as the sociologist Nathan Whetten notes in *Rural Mexico*, is that "farming is practised on hillsides so steep that it would be possible for a farmer to fall out of his field".

To a Mexican who draws his sustenance from this way of life, the

A morning sun lights the ramparts of the Chisos Mountains in Big Bend National Park, as the hills of Mexico lie in haze on the horizon.

name Sierra Madre—literally, mother range—must seem particularly apt. The origin of the name is, in fact, lost to history; one theory holds that it came from the way the Occidental and the Oriental, between them, cradle the country's high central plateau. Yet the same designation is given a third, smaller range far from the heartland—the Sierra Madre del Sur (Southern)—while, curiously, it is withheld from Mexico's highest mountains, the string of volcanoes that straddle the country horizontally just below Mexico City; presumably these peaks, 14,000 to 18,000 feet high, inspire more awe than simple filial respect. In any case, few Mexicans bother with the complexities of formal nomenclature. They call their ranges cordilleras, a word at once muscular and musical—and, to me, irresistibly inviting

I decided on Big Bend National Park as the jumping-off point for my trip into the Sierra Madre precisely because it is a microcosm, a kind of concentrated miniature, of northern Mexico. The term miniature, to be sure, is only relative; Big Bend encompasses 708,221 acres, and is the seventh largest national park in the contiguous United States. Within its boundaries, desert and mountains combine in a stark and dramatic landscape whose hazards are hinted at in some of the admonitions in the park's guidebooks for visitors. Don't poke around with snakes, tarantulas and scorpions. Carry a first-aid kit, including tweezers to pluck out cactus spines. Be careful of floods during the rainy season. If you become lost in the desert, arrange rocks every few miles to spell out HELP, with an arrow to show the direction you are headed in.

In fairness, it should be added that these admonitions appear in the guidebooks simply as sensible precautions to be taken in harsh country. For all the caveats, the appeal of the place is undeniable. The park's terrain sprawls and swoops, climbs and dives in myriad geometric patterns—domes, cliffs, mesas—with the Chisos Mountains in the centre and the Río Grande on the west, south and east. The wide curve the river makes on its 107-mile course along the southern boundary is what gave Big Bend its name. But the dominant impression the park gives is of a mad collage of angular lines: the jagged peaks of the mountains, the V shapes of the canyons, the spiky stalks of the desert flora.

To an Easterner used to neat shrubs and clipped hedges, the park's vegetation seems to be forever reaching out, poking up, leaning off in weird directions—imparting an abstract beauty to the scene and at the same time an air of menace. Big Bend's thorny garden of plants tends to generate metaphorical excess, often in the realm of weaponry. Spine

The pencil-thin stalks of a candelilla plant, 15 to 20 inches in height, capture the sun's rays along a tranquil stretch of the Río Grande.

encrusted, bristly and tough, they remind a newcomer of lances, swords and daggers—sometimes all too vividly. Climbing a boulder in a Big Bend canyon shortly after sunset, I reached out for support and slapped my hand down firmly on the pad of a blind prickly pear. I spent the next three days gingerly plucking tiny brown barbs, called glochidia, from my protesting flesh. At that I was lucky; in grazing areas outside the park, cattle that include the blind prickly pear in their diet sometimes get a face full of glochidia, and are blinded as a result.

On another hike I leaned back to rest against a rock and brushed against a hedgehog cactus. I managed to get my hand between my skin and the hedgehog's spines before I made full contact, thus sacrificing one paw to carelessness. This time it took two weeks for the spines to work themselves out, but again I consoled myself that things could have been worse; the spines could have come from a lechuguilla. This variety of agave, found nowhere else in the world but the Chihuahuan Desert region, is about as eye arresting as a plant can be. Out of a rosette of low-lying leaves it thrusts a narrow stalk as tall as 15 feet, topped when in bloom by red, orange, yellow or green flowers. But the leaves are tipped with spines so powerful that they can puncture a cowboy's thick boot or wound his horse. The agave lechuguilla is one of the main reasons why few of the park's horses have unscarred fetlocks.

Tender but wiser after my painful introduction to the arsenal of Big Bend's cacti, I turned my attention to a desert plant that appeared entirely innocuous—a perennial herb called candelilla, which looks something like asparagus and is very much at home on both sides of the Río Grande. It was a new species for me, and indeed harmless, but I soon learned that it generates a lot of trouble even so.

In Big Bend it is illegal merely to pick a candelilla, and in Mexico the federal government keeps a sharp eye on its growth. The reason is economic. To conserve moisture the candelilla stalks are coated with a wax that happens to be highly prized for use in shoe polish, chewing gum and floor wax. When the plant is ready for harvesting, it is pulled out of the ground whole and boiled in water with sulphuric acid added, whereupon the wax rises to the top and can be skimmed off. The operation requires very little equipment. While boating on the river one day I saw what local people call a wax factory, deserted for the winter, on the Mexican shore; it was no more than a series of cane-topped lean-tos huddled against a cliff. The wax fetches top prices in the United States; hence there is a temptation to smuggle it across—one kind of border traffic that nature cannot control.

In the end, what fascinated me most about the vegetation I saw was neither the cacti nor the candelillas but the profusion of grasses—chino and tobosa on the flats, bluestem and side-oats grama on the slopes. At first the sight of so much green comes as a shock to anyone accustomed to picturing desert terrain solely in terms of barren sands, baked dunes and dun colours. Then, belatedly, one recalls that by definition a desert is any place that generally averages less than 10 inches of rainfall each year. All manner of growing things can survive in such an environment—provided they have the ability, by one means or another, to conserve moisture.

The candelilla dons its waxy coat. Cacti hoard moisture in their spongy bodies. The ocotillo keeps water loss at a minimum by shedding its leaves in dry seasons. The yucca and the mesquite send down long roots to tap water sources deep in the earth. As for the grasses, their secret is the most elementary of all: they persist simply because they are hardy enough to endure extended periods of drought.

At Big Bend, as in most of the northern Sierra Madre, the rainfall is a feast-or-famine affair. In late summer and early autumn, sudden and ferocious thunderstorms unload as much as an inch of rain in an hour, cloudbursts slash the parched earth into hundreds of washes, and even the scruffiest cacti bloom more profusely, brightening the landscape with splashes of purple and yellow and red. Then, for much of the winter and spring, there is no rain at all. December, the month of my visit, averages a mere half inch.

Exploring the park at this dry time, I was hard put to imagine it covered by a vast sea. Yet that was its condition, according to geologists' estimates, 100 million years ago. Great masses of limy sediments, composed of microscopic plankton and the ancestors of today's shellfish, were deposited in the sea. Then, gradually, the main body of water receded, leaving swamps filled with dense vegetation.

By 75 million years ago Big Bend had a whole new look. It was now covered with ferns, mosses and water-loving trees, and a haven for dinosaurs, enormous crocodile-like beasts and winged reptiles. These giant creatures prevailed for about 10 million years before they became extinct—possibly because of a drastic change in climate—and the small mammals that had coexisted with them began to proliferate.

Some 70 million years ago, the Big Bend area underwent yet another transformation wrought by a protracted process of mountain building. The layers of limestone that had been deposited in the ancient sea were upended, broken into blocks, curved into loops and otherwise re-arranged by uplifting, faulting and folding. Some 15 million years later, molten material from the earth's interior squeezed upwards through the sedimentary rocks. Then further faulting and tilting tangled and interlocked the sedimentary and igneous rocks. An old Indian legend offers its own more romantic version of this process: when the Great Maker finished the earth and put stars in the sky and fish in the ocean, he had a big pile of rocks left over. He threw them all into one huge jumble and the result was Big Bend.

Through the millennia, rain and atmospheric gases have eaten away at the rocks. The intensity of the storms at Big Bend has helped to quicken the pace of erosion, and so has the Río Grande. In ancient times the river's passage was a relatively easy matter of penetrating the softer clay sediments that covered the rocks; but as these sediments trapped the Río Grande in its channel, the river had to slice its way through hard rock. As it went it carved a number of spectacular canyons out of limestone mesas. At Mariscal Canyon, at the park's southernmost point, the rock walls rise to a height of 1,800 feet above the river. At Santa Elena Canyon, 35 miles to the north-west of Mariscal, the gap in the mesa looks like an enormous gate inexplicably left open in the middle of a gigantic stone fence, and in fact a 19th-Century army officer named it Puerta Grande, Great Door.

Erosion and weathering at Big Bend have produced a dazzling variety of rock formations in rich hues of buff, deep brown, amber and lavender, and have also laid bare some of the park's primeval past. Embedded in rocks high on the Chisos peaks are the remains of pro-totypical snails, clams and oysters from the ancient sea. Though fossil hunting by amateurs is forbidden, paleontologists with special permission to roam Big Bend have unearthed traces of many dinosaurs and, in sedimentary rock that was laid down by an ancient stream, numerous bones of the flying reptiles called pterosaurs. They lived at the same time as the dinosaurs, flapping and gliding through the air on great batlike wings. The biggest of the Big Bend pterosaurs, according to the estimates of paleontologists, weighed nearly 200 pounds and had a wingspan of 36 to 39 feet—enough to qualify it easily as the largest flying creature yet discovered.

In time, other wonders may be yielded up by Big Bend's rocks. Their exposure through erosion and weathering is, of course, a continuing process, and one that gives Big Bend a tantalizing look of incomplete-ness. Dwight Deal, a geologist at the Chihuahuan Desert Research

Institute in Alpine, Texas, north of the park, told me that geologists can spend their entire careers poking around in Big Bend without completely understanding its details. "I've been here for more than seven years," he said, "and I'm just beginning to learn enough about the particulars of the geological framework of this country to use it as an effective teaching tool."

Big Bend did, in fact, see service as a rocky classroom of sorts when moon-bound astronauts were sent to the park to study its rock formations and contours. After this basic grounding, they were better able to report back to NASA on the geology of the moon.

Long before the geologists and astronauts and fossil hunters, nameless nomadic Indians roamed Big Bend. One of their early encounters with the white man is memorialized at Lost Mine Peak in the Chisos Mountains. Some 16th-Century Spanish explorers, the story goes, discovered gold on the mountain, took a number of the Indians prisoner, and forced them to work the mine. The Indians soon rebelled, and killed their captors; they then sealed the mine entrance to prevent further exploitation of their people. Though the location of the mine was later forgotten, a legend persists that if on Easter morning a searcher stands in the door of the chapel at Presidio San Vicente—an abandoned town on the Mexican side of the border—he will see the sun's first rays strike the exact mine entrance.

The first tribes to occupy Big Bend for more than brief periods were the Chisos and the Apache; ultimately the Apache drove out the Chisos and lived in the area until the 1880s. One of the last of the Apache was a chief named Alsate, who conducted frequent raids into Mexico and fought skirmishes with garrisons there. The Mexicans were never able to entrap him; he died, still eluding them, in a small cave on Pulliam Peak in the Chisos, not far from Lost Mine Peak. Another of Big Bend's enduring legends holds that when Alsate died, the contours of the mountain where he had made his last stand were suddenly transformed into an outline of the chief's defiant head.

But the real terrors of Big Bend—and of northern Mexico as well —were the nomadic Comanches. It had not taken the Comanches long to realize that the horse, reintroduced to North America by the conquistadors, would be of inestimable value to them in their travels around the plains of the south-west. Since horses were abundant in Mexico, the Comanches began crossing the Río Grande to steal them. The plunder continued, with some regularity, for more than 150 years until

Dense tufts of needle grass turn russet as the autumn dry season invades the Chisos Mountains in Big Bend National Park.

the mid-19th Century. By then the Comanches had a new reason to continue their forays across the border: the buffalo, upon which they depended heavily for food and other needs, was being systematically exterminated in the States. Every September large Comanche raiding parties would head across Big Bend, ford the Río Grande and gallop more than 500 miles south into Mexico, attacking ranches, stealing food and livestock and enslaving young Mexicans. The "Comanche moon" —September's full moon—signalled the start of the most dreaded time of the year for the Mexicans, and the pillaging lasted until November or December. The main Comanche trail, pitted by thousands of hoofs, was so clearly stamped on the Mexican land that it eventually became the border between the states of Chihuahua and Coahuila.

The United States Army finally subdued both Comanches and Apache in the late 19th Century, and cattle ranchers moved into Big Bend, there to remain until the establishment of the national park in 1944. One final flurry of violence took place in 1916, when the Mexican Revolution spilled across the river. A band of raiders attacked a small American garrison at Glenn Springs, some 10 miles inside the park's present south-eastern boundary. They killed three men and a boy, and the United States cavalry promptly fortified the post. Its only signs today are neat borders of rocks along vanished pathways and tent sites.

I spent my last few days at Big Bend exploring the Chisos Mountains, which are related to the Sierra Madre Oriental. Both ranges, along with an intervening cordillera called the Sierra del Carmen that flanks Big Bend on the east and continues down into Mexico, are topographically part of a vast discontinuous chain that begins with the Rockies to the north. All were created during the same mountain-building period 40 to 70 million years ago. Today, almost all the way down this chain, many of the same life forms—animal as well as plant—recur, even though they are in enclaves hundreds of miles apart.

I had seen much of Big Bend's plant life, but little of its animals. Most of them are nocturnal, thus avoiding both the heat of day and predation by man and other animals. Among the park's more skittish and seldom-seen mammals is a subspecies of white-tailed deer. Big Bend is, in fact, the only United States habitat of this shy and delicate creature, though it also lives across the border in the Sierra del Carmen, and is called the del Carmen whitetail. At 100 pounds, it is about one-third the size of the desert mule deer, and an easy prey for a fellow occupant of Big Bend, the cougar. Known also as the mountain lion or puma and locally dubbed the panther, the cougar weighs up to 160 pounds. Only about half a dozen of these fierce, tawny beasts are reported each year in the park; their nocturnal habits, as well as a fear of their own worst enemy, man, keep sightings rare.

My companion on the trip into the Chisos was George Burdick, who taught the children of park staff members during the school year and in summer worked as a park naturalist, guiding visitors around. Burdick gave me a quick rundown on Big Bend's wildlife, and I felt we were off to a good start when he expressed some cautious optimism about our chances of seeing one or two of its representatives.

Our first goal was a hidden canyon in the Chisos foothills, one of the few oases in the park that is verdant year-round. Our trail took us across shrub-dotted desert and then on an abrupt descent into a dry arroyo, where a single century plant bloomed in defiance of the season; it should have died in October, but the weather had stayed mild. As we moved up the arroyo, the vegetation thickened, a mass of prickly pear and sumac bushes and low-growing oaks. Finally we heard the sweetest sound in the desert, the musical ripple of running water. A thin spray of water trickled down a tiered wall of rock perhaps 300 feet high; at the bottom was a dark pool about 100 feet around, draining in a shallow creek that flowed for only a few dozen yards before it was swallowed by the thirsty soil. We paused at the pool and looked up at the rock wall; about halfway up we could see a tiny canyon wren, and a minute later we heard its song, starting high and plunging down the scale exactly as the water descended the rock.

Burdick checked the ground around the pool for tracks. "This is the only water in a pretty wide area," he said, "and there ought to be some customers here tonight—deer or javelina or maybe a bobcat. We probably won't see them but we might hear them." We moved back about 100 yards and took up watchful positions on top of a rock. We sat in silence in the enveloping dusk, trying not to move.

The first stars winked above the soaring silhouettes of the mountains. I felt a chill: the temperature would dip below 40° F. that night, though in this part of the world that is considered relatively warm for December. Suddenly we heard a faint noise in the bushes, the sound of twigs and leaves being brushed. "Might be a ring-tailed cat," Burdick whispered. But it fell quiet again. I shifted position and instantly worried that the swishing of my nylon parka would scare off any animal. Then we heard another soft step on dry leaves, closer this time, and aimed our flashlights. A startled racoon turned and bolted into a bush.

One of the five species of poisonous snakes at Big Bend, a black-tailed rattler flicks its tongue upon sensing an intruder. The snake's tongue aids its organs of smell by picking up chemical particles in the air and carrying them back to a set of unique sensory cells, located in the roof of the mouth, which transmits them to the brain.

Silence again. My ears were becoming attuned to it now, and I soon began to hear a series of faint brushing sounds. "Could be deer," Burdick said. But the sounds stopped. Maybe the deer sensed our presence, or maybe they were never there. Total animal count for the night: one racoon. As we climbed down from our observation post and hiked back out of the canyon to our campsite, I asked Burdick about the ring-tailed cat he had mentioned. "A member of the racoon family," he explained, "about the size of a half-grown house cat."

In the morning we headed into the higher reaches of the Chisos. Because of the altitude of the mountains, nearly 8,000 feet, they hold the few vestiges of the glacial age that survive in Big Bend. As the last Ice Age drew to an end, and the lower reaches of Big Bend warmed and dried out over the centuries, cold-climate trees such as ponderosa pine, cypress and quaking aspen gradually retreated to higher elevations. They remain there as oddities in an alien environment; seeing them, I found it hard to relate them to the desert vegetation flourishing below.

We climbed slowly up from the trail head in the Chisos Basin, an eroded bowl in the north-west part of the range, past splashes of red trumpetilla flowers and yellow damianitas. Both were blooming at least a month beyond their normal growing season in daytime temperatures of almost 70° F. Ahead of us, I suddenly saw my second animal of the trip: a stumpy, piglike creature of about 50 pounds with a shiny black coat, waddling off the trail. "Javelina," Burdick said. "They're all over this country. You usually smell them before you see them." Their distinctive musky essence, he explained, is emitted from a gland near the tail whenever they sense danger.

Seeing a single javelina, it turned out, was unusual. More often they travel in bands of up to 25 or more. They wear a grumpy expression, possibly because of their pronounced nearsightedness, which may also be the reason they race off madly in all directions when frightened.

Farther up the trail we passed a drooping juniper, a tree common in the Sierra Madre Occidental but found outside Mexico only in the Chisos. The drooping juniper has such a hangdog demeanour that many visitors to Big Bend believe that it must be dying. A slim tree, it grows no higher than 25 feet, and has light yellow-green leaves that dangle loosely from its branches. But it is highly adaptable, growing as well on dry slopes as it does in wet canyon bottoms. Peering at us from a branch of the juniper was a grey-breasted blue jay known as the Mexican jay; it, too, has strayed from Mexico as far as the Chisos.

In time we reached a notch on the side of the mountain we were climbing, 6,900-foot Ward Mountain, and came in sight of a tidy little canyon not more than 100 yards wide and about 200 yards deep. Though it gave way to another, larger canyon on its far side, it appeared to be an entity in itself, a self-contained environment. No water was visible —springs are rare in this particular part of the Chisos—but vegetation was abundant: alligator juniper, so called from the chequered texture of its bark; piñon pine; stilted century plants; evergreen sumac; grey-green prickly pear; mountain mahogany and dozens of other plants.

I wondered aloud what the wildlife population of this curious enclave might include. "It would mostly be nocturnal," Burdick replied. "Coyotes and bobcats are probably around here at night, and there might be a bobcat den on the hillside." There was not enough prickly pear to attract many javelinas, he added, but there was a plentiful supply of deer browse.

"There's probably seventy-five different kinds of critters living in here," Burdick said. "Rock squirrels, cottontail rabbits, brush mice, spiny lizards. There'll be maybe thirty species of snake, including a couple of rattlers in the summer. Ring-tailed cats. Skunks. You'll see this sort of wildlife community time and time again when you're in the northern Sierra Madre." What we saw now was a single cactus wren on an alligator juniper branch. The canyon was quiet except for the faint whooshing sound of the wind, and Burdick mused that canyons like this one might have been Indian camps as recently as a century ago.

We reached our own camp, an unmanned ranger cabin high in the mountains near Boot Spring, shortly before dusk and brewed up some freeze-dried stew for dinner. Then we went outside, and Burdick tried to summon up a coyote or bobcat with a plastic whistle-like caller.

While we waited, I asked Burdick if he had ever met a cougar in the Chisos. The closest he ever came, he said, was two years earlier, on the trail we had taken to Boot Spring. A group of park visitors had started off on horseback at eight one morning, and he started hiking along the same route at 9:30. "I found cougar tracks on top of the horse tracks," he recalled, "I was that close." He lost the tracks and later found them again on top of the ridge.

Burdick went on to tell me about two species—one plant, one animal—that I should come back to see in the spring or summer, after my trip to Mexico. They were, he explained, two more examples of species found outside Mexico only in the Big Bend region. The plant is the pitahaya, or strawberry cactus; it blooms only from April to July, and produces a tan pod about two inches across, which peels like a banana to reveal a delicious fruit much like the one that gives it its nickname.

Around the time the pitahaya begins to bloom the other species Burdick had in mind arrives in Big Bend—the colima warbler. These birds were unknown outside Mexico until 1928, when one of them was spotted near Boot Spring. Sparrow-sized, grey and yellow, colima warblers winter in the Sierra Madre Oriental, then fly north to nest and breed in the Chisos. But they are never numerous. In some years bird watchers taking a census have counted fewer than 100 in the Chisos.

The evening passed with no takers for Burdick's caller: even the coyote proved elusive. Finally we conceded defeat, and turned in.

The next morning we took the South Rim trail, which offers a magnificent panoramic view of the park, the Río Grande, and a large slice of northern Mexico. The day was clear, and we were about 7,000 feet above sea level. Mountains, long ridges, buff-coloured limestone cliffs and deep arroyos alternated in waves across the landscape. The terrain in the foreground resembled an enormous brown blanket with a dozen giant bobcats under it, bulging up in every imaginable shape. "It takes you three looks to see it," Burdick said. The Sierra del Carmen, blue and purple in the distance, dominated the view to the east. Santa Elena Canyon, one of the great canyons the Río Grande carved, lay 25 miles west. The river itself, 16 miles south of us, was a barely discernible ribbon of silver. Beyond it, on the horizon, the faint outlines of the first mountains of my next stop on this journey of exploration, the Sierra Madre Oriental, were visible through our binoculars.

Gateway to the Sierra Madre

For most of its 1,248-mile course as the border between Mexico and the United States, the Río Grande meanders quietly across sere deserts and gravelly grasslands that sweep away south to the Sierra Madre. About a third of the way on its journey to the Gulf of Mexico, however, the river abruptly plunges into a series of rocky defiles such as Santa Elena Canyon (right), whose walls rise 700 to 1,800 feet, quickening the river's pace and shutting out all but the noonday sun. There, at the southwest corner of Big Bend, the river is at its most intriguing, a waterway of varied moods and stark beauty.

The seasons contribute to the river's inconstancy. In late summer the Rio Grande—or Río Bravo, as it is known in Mexico—lives up to its name. Though the area gets only about eight inches of rain each year, nearly three-quarters of that falls from June to September. At this time the river may rise as much as 16 feet, although since 1914 its flow has been partly controlled by dams on the tributary Río Conchos, which drains part of the Sierra Madre Occidental and empties into the Río Grande from the south.

Swollen by summer rains, the Río Grande overflows its banks, ripping up miles of cane and reeds, rampaging through the canyons, and inundating enormous boulders that block the channel during the dry months (pages 46-47). Flash floods, roaring down from the mesas that line the river, surge unimpeded over the rock-strewn ground, stripping away the earth from beneath mesquite trees and other scrubby vegetation.

In the late autumn—when the photographs on the following pages were taken—the river shrinks down to more modest proportions, trickling over its rocky bed. Now reduced to an average depth of only about three feet, the water exposes sandy beaches and gravel bars that spread out as neatly as the surface of a suburban driveway. At this time, too, the remnant moisture of the recent rainy season finds a colourful expression in the still-blossoming riverside plants —salt cedar, esperanza and paper flowers. And the trickle of water through side canyons tops up the natural pools called tinajas that will serve as watering holes for animals over many months of drought.

This is an ideal time to view the river, for the evidence of its former violence is fully exposed to view. And yet its quiet side, the still beauty of the place, stands revealed.

Just inside the entrance to Santa Elena Canyon, the Río Grande glides between massive limestone walls composed of sediment laid down here millions of years ago when the whole region lay beneath a prehistoric sea. This type of sedimentary rock extends all the way south into the Sierra Madre Oriental.

The zigzag path of Santa Elena Canyon, beginning at the entrance cleft into the bluff (near left), cuts through a plateau of limestone known as Mesa de Anguila on the Texan side (foreground) and as Sierra Ponce in Mexico.

The ragged remnant of a stone wall, built as a simple water-control device, stands on top of a mesa near a canyon rim of the Río Grande. The wall, flanked by spiky torrey yuccas and the pads of a prickly-pear cactus, was probably erected by local Indians to divert runoff from infrequent rains.

A deep pothole, or tinaja, in the floor of a narrow side canyon holds water left from the rainy season. Tinajas result if waterborne pebbles collect in a depression in a rock over which runoff periodically flows; after a long time swirling around in the runoff, the pebbles grind out a hole.

A tough, old mesquite tree (left) clings to the earth wall of a Río Grande side canyon. Run-off surging through the arroyo has exposed some of the roots without managing to dislodge the tree. A tenacious survivor in the dry land along the river and south into the Sierra Madre, the mesquite sometimes sends down taproots as deep as 100 feet in search of ground water.

At low ebb in November, the Río Grande (right) roils around an exposed gravel bar. Less than three feet deep and only about 60 feet wide at this point, the river swells threefold during summer floods, when it will bear most of these rocks farther downstream.

A quiet vestige of the river's power, this beach at the base of a buttressed canyon wall is formed of rock particles from the area. During summer rains, sediment washes down from the uplands, eventually to be deposited along the shores as the flood recedes. The next flood may wash it away.

A maze of broken carrizo, a reed that grows along the Río Grande, lies where floodwaters have deposited it on a ledge above the river. Left to dry in the desert air, such mounds of carrizo may remain for years as the sign of a particularly rainy season that swelled the river to an unusual height.

The Rockslide, a quarter-mile-long
labyrinth of limestone boulders
sheared off from the Mexican side of
Santa Elena Canyon, constricts the
flow of the river at low water. Dimples
on the boulders' surfaces record the
abrading action of rocks that are swept
along by the river when it is in flood.

A salt-cedar bush swells with blooms in the late-autumn sunshine at the foot of a canyon cliff. A member of the desert-loving tamarisk family, the salt cedar readily takes root in thin, sandy soil near streams and rivers, where it crowds out most other plants.

The trumpet-shaped flowers of an esperanza brighten a canyon slope 80 feet above the Río Grande. Found as far south as Argentina, the plant grows in many places in the Sierra Madre and adjacent desert regions. Here it is near the northern end of its range.

The gleaming thread of the Río Grande, seen below the horizon from a point about three miles inside Mexico at the edge of Sierra Madre

country, snakes across a rocky landscape spotted with clumps of chino grama grass, prickly-pear cactus and yellow paper flowers.

2/ The Dark Heart of the Cordillera

*These men dared to descend to a region where
the whole of nature is reversed.* SENECA/ *QUESTIONS OF NATURE*

Ten feet inside the cave entrance, I waited a long minute to let my eyes adjust to the dark. I was near the top of a talus slope that fell about 100 feet to the floor of the most enormous room I had ever been in. Several little cones of light moved eerily across the floor. The lights, faint and filmy, as if they were under water, came from the carbide lamps carried by the vanguard of our eight-member party. They appeared to be drifting through some surrealistic nether world, without perspective or norms of measurement.

Dwight Deal nudged me and we started down the slope. For the entire previous day, Deal had been telling me about this cave called Gruta del Palmito, 75 miles north-west of the city of Monterrey in the Sierra Madre Oriental. But the fact of it so transcended my imaginings that I felt vaguely embarrassed. I normally subtract 25 per cent from any superlative I hear, on principle; in this case such scepticism seemed shamefully small-minded. "Cave explorers talk about the Sierra Madre Oriental with the same wild glow in their eyes that mountaineers have when they mention the Himalayas," Deal had said. "For a novice like you to begin with Gruta del Palmito. . . . " He searched for an analogy. "It's, well, it's like doing your first climb on Kanchenjunga."

Nevertheless, there I was, just inside the cave now, struggling with the presence of this vast and dark chamber and trying to perceive its limits. But even though my eyes were adjusting and the light of my own carbide lamp punched the blackness, I could not see how far the room extended in any direction. Deal had given me the dimensions —150 feet wide, 525 feet long, 100 feet high—but numbers can be feeble tools of communication. The analogies I tried were not much better. I thought of the largest rooms I had ever seen—a cathedral in Italy, a dirigible hangar in California. But this room was something apart, its scope beyond my experience. And it was just the entrance chamber. The main room well beyond turned out to be the same height, but ranging from 200 to 400 feet in width and a full 1,600 feet long. The depth of the cave, from the entrance to its lowest point, is 667 feet.

There was another element about the cave that was new and strange —the sense of disorientation it gave me. I learned later that this is an emotion experienced by all first-time cave explorers. It soon passes, I was told, and one begins feel more or less at home, but it stayed with me for the duration of my underground ventures in the Sierra Madre Oriental. It is as if your sensory perceptions are no longer reliable: you don't see quite as well, the things you touch don't have the texture you expect, sound is distorted, you're not altogether certain where you're putting your feet.

Gruta del Palmito—in English, Grotto of the Little Palm—derives its name from a small, scruffy tree at the cave entrance. The Gruta region is an object of study for the Chihuahuan Desert Research Institute, which Dwight Deal runs. The institute has a broad charter to examine geological, zoological, botanical, archaeological and other scientific aspects of the desert throughout north-central Mexico. As it happens, the Sierra Madre Oriental is one of the world's most spectacular areas of caverns and pits. Deal and other veteran cavers regard all these holes in the earth as caves—both those that can be walked into and those that must be descended by rope—and they estimate that there are more than 1,000 known caves in the Oriental. Deal assured me that an excursion to some of them would be rewarding both as unalloyed adventure and as a study of what he called underground plumbing, the system of water-carved passages inside the mountains.

My first view of the Oriental had been a glimpse of its northernmost foothills from the South Rim trail of Big Bend. A few days before my descent into Gruta del Palmito, I took a closer look at the entire northern part of the range from a small aircraft. North of Monterrey the Oriental is a series of discontinuous mountains, 5,000 to 8,000 feet high. The climate is arid in the lowlands of this region, and the most common plants are the same dry-country species that thrive in Big Bend

—prickly pear, lechuguilla, creosote bush, yucca, ocotillo, mesquite. Some of the same animals that tenant Big Bend—coyote, bobcat and cougar—patrol the washes and the tan hills.

Around Monterrey the look of the Oriental changes. The mountains rise dramatically, jutting up in a great wall to the west and south of the city. Just as dramatically, the range broadens here, spreading westwards in a 100-mile-wide succession of ridges. When I asked one Mexican friend in Monterrey where a particular mountain was, he pointed vaguely towards the west and replied, "Seven ridges from here". Though towns and villages dot the range, some are reachable only by burro.

The Oriental varies as much from east to west as it does from north to south. The westernmost slopes rise more gently, almost imperceptibly, from the Chihuahuan Desert. Farther to the east the dominant sandy desert hues begin to give way to light green scrub and, still farther, to dark green; here pine forests start to crowd the ridges and mountaintops. The eastern flank of the range, less than 200 miles from the Gulf of Mexico, forms a steep escarpment, the antithesis of the gentle western slopes. Its pine forests, nourished by the precipitation that is borne in from the gulf by the prevailing north-east trade winds, are the richest green of all.

The real fascination of the Oriental, however, lies underground. Most of the range is composed of limestone, a soluble rock originally deposited as marine sediment—shells, coral and the remains of other sea life and masses of inorganic lime mud. The most porous and most easily dissolved variety of limestone is reef rock, and this abounds in the Sierra Madre Oriental, along with other kinds that are vulnerable to water action only along weaknesses—fractures, fissures and spaces between grains in the rock.

Rain seeks out these weaknesses and attacks with a modest but highly effective arsenal of chemicals. As rainwater falls, it picks up some carbon dioxide from the air and much more from decaying vegetable and animal matter in the soil it passes through. By the time the rain seeps into the limestone below it has become a weak solution of carbonic acid; but weak as it is, it has the power to dissolve the limestone, leaving water-filled holes and—once they are drained—the roofed caves as well as the deep open pits that local Mexicans and most scientists call sótanos.

Ultimately, the rain plus limestone plus tropical warmth have combined in the Oriental to produce an intriguing kind of jumbled topography known as karst, after an Adriatic region where it is also prominent. In a karst region the limestone terrain is riddled with sinkholes and other signs of collapsed surface; and since almost all water in such country drains away underground, rivers and streams are notably absent.

In the southern Oriental, karst is still forming. This part of the range lies below the Tropic of Cancer, where temperatures are high; moreover, rainfall is abundant—up to 100 inches annually in some places —since the range at this point is only 75 miles from the Gulf of Mexico. The northern Oriental was once as warm and wet as the southern Oriental, but global climatic changes have left it much drier, and its karst landscape has been worn down by surface erosion. But the north still contains relict caves such as Gruta del Palmito, which lured me underground for the first time.

Deal and I moved carefully down the talus slope until we reached the bottom of the entrance chamber. The floor was littered with dozens of huge, squarish boulders, some about 20 by 40 feet, which cavers call breakdown—chunks that have broken off the ceiling or walls along fractures that widened as the limestone was dissolved. Shiny, round little rocks, ranging from the size of a pea to one foot in diameter, glistened between the boulders. "Those are cave pearls," Deal said. He explained that as water seeps down through the cave's limestone, it becomes heavily laden with the mineral calcite. Relentless dripping over the years creates basin-like depressions in the cave floor. Calcite sticks to fine grains of sand from the cave floor that have collected in the basins. Once the pearls form, further dripping rolls them around until they are smooth and highly polished, and they are usually a lustrous pinkish white in colour.

We caught up with the rest of our group and headed for the far side of the chamber. We were an odd assortment—a printer, a landscaper, a bookkeeper, two students, an archaeologist, a geologist (Deal) and me. Most were Texans who had driven much of the previous night to get in a weekend of cave exploring, an avocation they pursue with the disciplined ardour of religious novitiates.

We made our way along a wall whose vertical, reddish-brown stripes made it look like a huge, rippled curtain of bacon; the colour, Deal said, came from a mineral, iron oxide, that had been dissolved in water and precipitated out. Beyond the wall a passageway led towards another high-ceilinged chamber. I was trying very hard to retain a sense of direction, distance and proportion, but I felt myself losing it as we weaved past boulders, through rock tunnels, and in and out of alcoves where ceilings and walls were sometimes close enough to see, sometimes lost in the shadows.

Calcite was evident here, too. Stalactites hung like icicles from the ceilings and their companion structures, stalagmites, poked up from the floors. Where they met they formed columns, each of them one more obstacle to get round. In cave parlance such formations are called decorations; these happened to be a waxy white, though as we moved deeper into the cave we were to see them in far brighter colours and ever more fanciful shapes.

The footing was often slippery, sometimes steep. My hard hat rode unsteadily on a head unaccustomed to cover, and I was perspiring freely. The temperature in the cave was perhaps 75° F., about 20° warmer than it was outside, and humid; because rock is a good insulator, cave temperatures are not usually subject to surface variations, remaining constant the year round.

We still had a way to go to reach the cave's main chamber. The approach to it began at a ledge in which earlier cavers had cut steps. The ledge is known as Paso de Muerte—Pass of Death—because of its perils. It is only a foot wide; on one side of it is a wall, on the other side a pit about 100 feet deep. I leaned into the wall and made my way across. Someone in our party had mentioned that children from the near-by village of Bustamante make a torch-lit pilgrimage every year to an altar deep in the cave's interior. I envisioned this column of little torch-bearers stepping carefully across the Paso de Muerte, surrounded by eerie stalactites and stalagmites, and thought about Orpheus and Heracles and other mythical figures bearing the shadows of the underworld.

Beyond the ledge lay a long breakdown slope—an obstacle course of more huge boulders—that fell away into borderless darkness. The slope dropped 325 feet, nearly half of the cave's total depth, at an angle of 30°, and our carbide lamps illuminated only part of the way down. After I descended about 100 feet, I could not help thinking about the return climb back up.

There was something else that was beginning to bother me. Here and there I had already noticed some distinctly unattractive signs of man's presence in the cave, such as graffiti scratched on the walls. Worse yet, I had seen some of the cave's delicate formations broken off, obviously by hand. I commented to one of my companions about the defacement. He nodded angrily, and said that even though the government's permission is required to enter this cave or any other

An icicle-like formation of calcium carbonate decorates a rock surface inside the cave complex called Gruta del Palmito. The dazzling white mineral is precipitated out of water seeping through the limestone bedrock. The rust colour of the rock surface is caused by iron-bearing minerals.

cave in Mexico, vandalism continues to be a problem. It struck me as a deplorable way to treat a national treasure like Gruta del Palmito.

Fortunately, some of the more inaccessible areas of the cave have escaped unscathed. At one point, a few of us made our way through a low passage into a room about four feet high, small enough for our combined lights to fill it. Since few people had been in this room, only an occasional footprint marred its pristine beauty. The ceiling was a maze of forms of every imaginable shape, in colours ranging from white to gold and orange to reddish brown. Delicate butterscotch-and-white calcite icicles hung from it, interspersed with long, hollow tubes that cavers call soda straws. There were also chunks of hanging rock that looked like carrots, pineapples and cornhusks bunched together, and a tangled mass of white rock that resembled the underside of a deserted shrub, its roots grasping thirstily in all directions. Slender, elegant columns reached from floor to ceiling. I thought of the term cave decorations, and decided that it was something of an understatement.

In another alcove, the sight was equally breathtaking. Only one of our party had been in this room before; the others, myself included, stared open-mouthed at a succession of elegant little crystal formations on the wall: tiny, glassy needles called crystal points, projecting from orange-coloured, velvety-looking flowstone. Somebody was reminded of a coral reef formation, and the image did not seem at all far-fetched.

As we emerged from the alcove, we found other members of our party staring up at a nearly vertical side wall. Ron Ralph, the archaeologist, had started to climb the cave wall to see if there was an upper-level chamber. Finding none, he got stuck on his way down about 20 feet above the floor. He was having difficulty seeing the natural hand-holds and footholds he had used on his ascent, and the other cavers were talking him down.

"There's a good handhold about ten inches down from your left hand, Ron. . . . " Ralph lowered the hand, probing with his fingers. "I can't get the angle of it," he said. "Okay, okay," another caver said. "There's a foothold just down to the right of your right foot." Ralph found it, then moved his left hand to the lower hold. "What do I do now?" he said.

"Scream and jump," a caver joked. Ralph laughed; then his carbide lamp went out. Deal moved closer and aimed his light upwards. "This is the only way to help a caver," the man next to me whispered. "You can't catch him if he falls, and if you try to break his fall you wind up with two injured instead of one. He has to get down himself."

As it turned out, Ralph—an experienced rock climber as well as caver —was never in serious danger of falling. He made it down in another minute, jumping the last few feet. He brushed himself off and smiled self-consciously. "Sorry, folks," he said.

We continued on down the long breakdown slope, scrambling from boulder to boulder and skidding every so often on slippery rocks. At the bottom we wound through several stalactite-stalagmite columns until we dropped down still another slope, a small one—and there, before us, was the vast main room of Gruta del Palmito.

Like the entrance hall, it was too big to see all at once; its edges blurred into blackness. The villagers of Bustamante had placed their altar at one end of this room. A hand-hewn wooden table and several icons were set in front of a 40-foot-high curtain of white flowstone, another calcite formation of surpassing beauty; it looked like a limestone version of a lava flow. As we stood there admiring it, our voices sounded thin and reedy in the void.

There was one more objective to be reached, and we crossed to the far end of the room. At the base of a high wall was a hole that seemed to me to be barely wide enough for a cocker spaniel to get through. Beyond it a kind of chute about 30 feet long dropped down under a low ceiling. I watched as the first members of our party began to manoeuvre through the hole, slanting their shoulders and moving one part of the body at a time. My confidence, which had regained some lost ground on the downhill scramble, started to slip away again.

Then it was my turn. I took off my hat and my day pack and launched myself head first into the hole. My shoulders made it through all right, but sections to the south kept getting stuck. Each time I strained and wriggled and got free, I felt my pants slide lower down my hips. I demolished a ball-point pen in my trousers pocket and ripped a good wool shirt. Towards the end of the crawl way I found myself wriggling along on my back with my feet on the ceiling; for some reason I made better progress that way. At last I emerged, dusty, half-dressed and somersaulting, to the amused approval of my companions. I felt as though I had passed a formidable initiation rite.

We were now in the deepest chamber in the cave, more than 2,000 feet from the entrance. The room was the size of a tennis court, with a low ceiling, sloping floor, and orange flowstone walls. We stayed there until someone looked at his wristwatch and discovered that it was past three o'clock. We still had a three-hour trek to get back out of the cave—starting with the crawl way. "Just remember," Deal said, "if you get stuck, the rest of us behind you are stuck too." I got back through, this time the only casualty a pin in my watch.

On the long climb back I kept thinking about that crawl way, and it occurred to me that the apprehension I had felt was not so much a fear I would not make it as a fear I might *think* I could not make it. The thought was more alarming than the reality. Caves seem to touch some buried impulse in all of us. Perhaps they strum an atavistic chord that our conscious minds cannot hear. Almost everyone has some interest in caves, feels some attraction to them and yet some revulsion. Perhaps this ambivalence had been at the root of my sense of uneasiness upon entering the cave. Still, for all my concern, the slippery footing, the fear of fear itself, by the time I emerged I felt that this had been one of the supremely satisfying days of my life.

As I caught my breath outside Gruta del Palmito, I realized belatedly that something had been missing. I knew that caves harbour an astonishing variety of life; James Reddell, a Texas biologist, estimates that there are approximately 2,000 different species of cave fauna in Mexico alone. Yet I had seen none inside the cave. My companions explained that Gruta del Palmito is not noted for its fauna, and that the life that does exist there is so minute I would have had to hunt long and carefully to see it. Small frogs dwell in the ferns and lichens at the entrance; within the dark zone that begins 50 to 100 feet inside the cave, there are spiders, millepedes, beetles, daddy longlegs, and camel crickets—wingless crickets that live only in caves and other damp, dark places. But certain other typical cave denizens seem to be absent—blind cave fish, crayfish, snails and salamanders. The most conspicuous absentee is the commonest cave creature of Mexico, the bat.

I was to have better luck, at least so far as the bats were concerned, one afternoon a few days later in another cave, a small one near Linares, south of Monterrey. I went there accompanied by a young Mexican biology instructor specifically to see a species of bat that I had previously met only in horror tales—the vampire. This cave marks the northern limit of the species, which ranges all the way southwards to central Argentina and central Chile.

As we approached the entrance, my companion anticipated the question he knew I was bound to ask—about the vampire's notorious penchant for drinking blood. Quite true, he said. The creatures sleep during the day, then fan out shortly after dark to feed on the blood of burros, cows, dogs, horses and other animals. They approach their prey stealthily, alight and, as deftly as surgeons, remove a microscopically thin slice of skin with their razor-sharp incisors. As blood oozes up to the surface of the wound the vampire sucks it in, as through a straw, via a pair of grooves in the tongue. The victim, usually sleeping, rarely awakens as the bat drinks its fill.

The adult vampire, which weighs no more than an ounce and a half, consumes its weight in blood every 24 hours. The open wound it inflicts may look frightening, since such wounds clot more slowly than stablike punctures, but the excision is not painful and the amount of blood lost minor. The danger lies in the diseases the vampires transmit: murrina, a blood parasite deadly to cattle and horses; and the universally feared killer of animals and humans, rabies.

Inside the cave, we stepped around pools of guano that smelled strongly of ammonia, and pointed our flashlights at the ceiling, from which emanated a chorus of chittering squeaks. The light revealed a mass of about 200 vampires clustered in a recess in the domelike ceiling. My guide estimated that this was about half the cave's current bat numbers, though not necessarily an indication of the future population. The gestation period of these tiny mammals ranges from three to five months, and the females can get pregnant twice a year.

As we watched, some of the bats, a red-brown colour, with snub-nosed flat faces and pointed ears, scudded nervously along the ceiling and walls. A large group moved off and began to fly up and down the cave's 12-foot-wide corridor. The force of their wings fanning the air turned the cave into a wind tunnel. My companion pulled me against a wall to give them room to pass, and just then a bat bumped my leg. "They usually don't bite humans," he said, "unless you try to handle them." We turned off our lights and the sound of rushing wind immediately began to subside.

My ultimate objective in the southern Oriental was a terrifyingly deep hole in the ground known as Sótano de las Golondrinas, the Pit of the Swallows—actually a misnomer, since the birds that inhabit the pit are swifts and parakeets. Only a few skilled cavers, using nylon ropes, have ever descended into this *sótano*. Measuring the depth from the lowest point on the rim to the point directly below it on the bottom, they arrived at a figure of 1,091 feet. In fact, at one point the floor of the shaft is 1,306 feet deep, and passages extend below that to a depth of more than 1,700 feet. "Golondrinas is so big it's hard to appreciate," Dwight Deal told me. "You have to drop a rock and watch it start to

The plant known in Mexico as mala mujer—bad woman—spreads broad leaves to a shaft of sunlight in its forest habitat. Deceptively harmless in appearance, mala mujer's leaves, stalks and fruit contain a corrosive fluid that, on contact with human skin, causes a sting as virulent as a wasp's and intense pain for several hours.

wobble and float before you realize the scale. Or you lean over the rim and see what looks like a fly coming up and then it turns out to be a green parakeet."

Deal, Ron Ralph and I set out for Golondrinas on a warm morning in early January. Our starting point was Ciudad Valles, 100 miles below the Tropic of Cancer, and as we hiked south-west through the mountains I became aware of the sharp differences between this part of the Oriental range and its northern reaches. Now we were in a rain forest, lush and lively and thick with foliage. Yet the soil that spawns this abundant verdure is curiously shallow; it barely covers the limestone beneath. The ground is more rock than dirt—trees send their roots down through cracks in the limestone—and streams are rare even though rainfall is heavy. In fact, all the classic conditions of a well-developed karst landscape are present, including the great vertical shafts of the *sótanos*.

To get to Golondrinas we had to hike over two ridges and part way up a third, travelling a rocky trail that natives of the roadless region had cut through the forest. For the first few hours the trail slanted sharply upwards. We laboured along under our packs, drinking in the sensory delights of the jungle: bright orange and blue butterflies; olive-coloured *chachalacas*, birds about the size of bantam chickens, cackling to match their names; lazy-leafed banana trees; an unidentifiable swarm of green-leafed shrubs crowding the trailside. It was an inhabited jungle, to be sure. People and burros moved along the trail, packing coffee beans to the village of Aquismón where the paved road from Ciudad Valles ends and returning with water and supplies. We passed tin-roofed huts walled with untrimmed branches. A farmer's fat turkey sat in mid-trail and refused to budge. Three boys came by with burlap bags full of wood. "*Buenos dias*," they said cheerfully.

Deal pointed out a trickle of water emerging from between two boulders. "Springs crop up along the faults in uplifted limestone," he explained. "Most every village is built near such a spring; otherwise the water problem is pretty rough." He leaned down and plucked a small plant from the ground. Its root spread almost horizontally through perhaps an inch of earth. "See how shallow the soil is? This whole tropical garden is growing on about that much soil."

A black-and-white-striped millepede inched across the trail. Farther along a battalion of harvester ants marched solemnly by in parade formation, some of them carrying tiny triangular patches of green leaves that fluttered like military flags. A small, raucous band of bright-green parrots, each about a foot long, flew past. At least, I thought they were parrots, until my friends informed me that the birds were parakeets, possibly the ones that lived in our *sótano*.

We camped that night in a thatch-roofed, open-sided shelter at the intersection of two trails, awakening to a thick morning mist that soon cleared to reveal an astonishing spectacle. Parakeets were soaring by us in groups of two, three and four, their brilliant-green bodies lustrous in the sunlight. All around them, flying at high speed, were great swarms of black swifts. The residents of Sótano de las Golondrinas were off in search of their daily bread. I could see now why these white-throated swifts might have been mistaken for swallows. Though their wings are more scythelike, their size—no more than six inches long—and their markings are similar to those of some swallows, with touches of white at the throat, breast and on the rump.

We hoisted our backpacks and started up the trail, passing an occasional hut with a yard full of dark-red coffee berries drying in the sun. Here and there the undergrowth had been cleared, exposing jagged, pitted pinnacles of limestone. A strong baritone voice was singing a love song somewhere beyond the trailside shrubs. Two women passed, carrying pails of water on their heads.

I expressed my surprise at all the evidences we were seeing of human habitation. "Mexicans and Americans differ in their concepts of wilderness," Deal explained to me. "Mexicans can't afford to let any resources go untouched, even in wilderness areas like this one. All the land we're passing through is privately owned, with individual plots of up to ten acres.

"Remember," he went on, "not all wilderness is above ground. Underground areas can be considered true wilderness areas even if the surface land is put to economic use. Every underground resource in Mexico, caves included, is government owned. That's why we had to get permission to go into Gruta del Palmito, and we're also going to need it to visit Golondrinas."

At midday we arrived at the village where we were to secure the permission from the local *juez*, or judge, only to learn from his wife that he was in another village farther along our route. But we tarried awhile. Children surrounded us, the bravest reaching out to touch our backpacks. "*Vengan hay gringos aquí*," they called to their friends, summoning them to see the *norteamericanos*.

The two dozen structures that constituted the village were snuggled

A flight of green parakeets (above) wings past a limestone wall inside the awesome pit called Sótano de las Golondrinas (right), where they roost each night on ledges and in crevices. The walls of the pit—which also houses huge flocks of swifts—plunge more than a quarter of a mile from the tree-fringed rim to the bottom.

serenely if somewhat precipitously near the top of a ridge along one of the spring-producing faults. We sat down in the placid square and drank lukewarm soft drinks. A venerable Huastec Indian, barefoot and wearing a one-piece white garment, nodded gravely at us. Well on in years, he bore the strong features that distinguish his people. "Interesting thing about the Huastecs," Ralph said. "They are Catholics now, but they retain their belief in a deity known as Earth Owner, and think that he lives in a cave."

Late that afternoon, having found the judge and received his written approval for our venture, we started up the side of our third and last ridge—the one in which Golondrinas lies. In the hazy distance we could see the flat, green plain spreading eastwards to the Gulf of Mexico. Eager to reach the *sótano* before the sun went down, we stepped up our pace and virtually galloped the last half mile. Suddenly a huge black cloud blocked out the sun—the swifts, thousands of them, were swirling around in a vast circle. We were hell-bent now, stumbling through the underbrush looking for short-cuts to the pit, knowing that the swifts were circling it prior to roosting for the night. I became conscious of a loud, continuous whooshing sound, the noise of thousands of pairs of wings beating the air.

At last we came out of a forest of sweet gum and oak, and there, only a few yards ahead of us down a 10° slope, was the lip of the pit itself. Swifts were dive bombing into it by the hundreds, hurtling past us with such speed that they were little more than black blurs. The entire scene was one huge sensory explosion: the great clouds of birds, the rush of air as they roared into the pit, the jungle around its edges and the pit itself—dark and seemingly fathomless. We dropped to our knees and crawled cautiously to the overhanging edge. The bordering rock was fissured and pitted with crevices, so it was possible to wedge a foot or a knee and feel reasonably, though by no means totally, secure. I felt as if I were at the edge of a sloping roof on the Empire State Building.

As the swifts continued to circle in huge swarms, then swoop, I tried to make out the bottom of the pit. "What's on the floor?" I asked. "Guano," Ralph said.

During our frantic scramble to get to the pit, we had all picked up rocks. Now Ralph pulled out a stop-watch and Deal dropped the first rock. It fell straight down, then appeared to wobble and drift before it disappeared from sight. Ralph pressed the watch button when we heard a resonant *thunk*. "Ten-point-three seconds," he said. We tried again: 10.5. And again: 10.8. A flat rock went down in 12.7 seconds. I was getting a lesson in basic physics: different shapes of rock encounter variations in air resistance, with the result that they differ in the velocity at which they fall.

The storm of swifts was finally beginning to abate, and now we noticed the parakeets, chattering noisily. They had simply been waiting their turn. Little groups of them—from three to 10—appeared out of the trees and began making long, lazy loops around the top of the pit. They spiralled downwards in easy stages, their shiny, almost fluorescent green plumage growing dimmer and dimmer until they were specks in the dark tube. Half a dozen groups were in the air at any one time; when they had all entered the pit, half a dozen more showed up. The parakeets were more sedate than the swifts. It was as if the swifts were the children, the parakeets were the teachers and the end-of-recess bell had just rung, summoning all of them back into the schoolhouse.

How many birds live in this pit? How many leaves has the forest? The scene was mesmerizing, a glimpse of nature at its wildest and most beautiful. "I'd kind of like to go down there," Ron said quietly. Both he and Deal had the know-how to make the 1,100-foot free fall, but they had not brought the equipment. A free fall is a descent by rope in which the rope hangs completely free of the walls of the hole, and the caver dangles like a spider on a thread. Climbing in and out of a pit such as Golondrinas requires a tremendous amount of rope rigged through a metal brake rack to control speed, a sling harness and movable foot loops for the arduous climb up and out.

Golondrinas is not a straight, cylindrical shaft, as it appears from the rim, but bells out as it descends. At the top, its dimensions are about 160 feet by 205 feet, at the bottom, 440 feet by 1,000 feet—a floor area about six acres in size. "The first caver who got to the bottom in 1967 was amazed at how big it was," Deal said. "He wandered around for a while and then discovered he had lost sight of the end of his climbing rope. He finally got back to it after finding his own footprints and retracing them."

Ralph mentioned an even more unnerving experience he himself had undergone at another *sótano*. Together with several other cavers, he had obtained what the group thought were all the necessary permissions from local officials. But because of a misunderstanding caused by some confusing instructions in Spanish, they had inadvertently failed to contact one minor functionary. Angry that his permission had not been sought, he ordered the climbing rope to be pulled up while Ralph and his companion were on the bottom. They remained there for several hours before another official intervened and the rope was redropped. "When that rope hit the ground we were on it," Ralph recalled. "We kept bumping into each other on the way and it only took us a half hour to get up." A normal, unhurried ascent, he estimated, would have taken a couple of hours.

I asked Deal to tell me just how an outside pit like Golondrinas came to be. He explained that it originated when ground water seeped downwards at the intersection of a major fault and an exceptionally well-developed zone of vertical fractures in the rock. The limestone was gradually dissolved and small openings in it were enlarged, forming a big, water-filled underground chamber. The water in this ever-growing chamber continued to percolate downwards along the fissures, dissolving the limestone as it went. The amount of limestone removed by solution to form the main shaft of Golondrinas, Deal estimated, was an almost incredible 200 million cubic feet—five times the volume of Gruta del Palmito.

Golondrinas probably became an open pit after the water drained and the original chamber ceiling collapsed and blocks of its walls fell in, filling the bottom with hundreds of feet of breakdown. Today relatively little surface water enters the pit, though a small waterfall issues from one side of it after heavy rains. But, cavers report, the blocks on the pit floor appear to be dissolving. "It seems that this pit and others in the area are still growing deeper," Deal said. "The next generation of cavers may have to bring even longer ropes."

As we talked, the bird show ended, reminding us abruptly that it was nearly dark. We pitched our tents in a grassy clearing about 100 yards from the pit. "Watch out for the *mala mujer*; it's all over," Ralph said as we gathered wood. *Mala mujer* (in English, bad woman) is probably the most-avoided plant in Mexico, a narrow-trunked, 10-foot shrub with spiny hairs on its leaves and stalks that cause a stinging rash fiercely painful to the skin.

The next morning we awoke just after sunrise to a tornado of swifts zooming 30 feet above our tents. We dressed and hurried to the edge of the pit. The swifts were exploding out of the shaft like rocks from an erupting volcano. Peering over the lip, we could hear the wind from their wings echoing in the hole. The birds were shooting straight up and out, then swarming together and taking off eastwards, whizzing close over the tops of the trees.

We were so absorbed in the spectacle that at first we failed to notice a teenage boy standing on a near-by boulder. He was holding a long, flat stick and swatting at the swifts as they emerged; the stick made a sharp, whipping sound as he swung it, leaning precariously over the pit's edge. After a few minutes he climbed down to where we were. In one hand he held a single swift—the morning's harvest. He told us that he came here every morning and that he killed two or three birds a day on the average. I asked if anyone had ever fallen in; he said he had heard that another boy had fallen, 20 years ago.

"Why do you kill the birds?" Deal asked.

"To eat. There is no other reason," he replied.

Now the parakeets were beginning to glide gracefully out of the pit. They were leisurely; their long, spiralling flight pattern seemed much less compulsive than that of the swifts. They moved slowly into the day, pausing on the limb of a cliffside shrub to screech among themselves before flying off lazily. The youthful bird hunter showed no interest in them; they were clever enough to elude his stick.

More parakeets kept coming out for 20 or 30 minutes before the place fell quiet again. A tiny hummingbird hovered a few feet out over the pit. I wondered if it realized where it was. Then, with a sudden explosion, another flock of swifts shot out of the pit. Late sleepers? The clean-up detail? They had waited for the parakeets to complete their exodus before they took off.

We squirmed along the sloping rock for a final look into the *sótano*. It was silent, a huge dark city now emptied of its commuting citizens. Morning sunlight moved slowly down the western wall. I wondered what the first Indian to come across this pit had thought about it. Maybe he thought it was Earth Owner's house. Maybe it is.

NATURE WALK / **In Cuatro Ciénegas Basin**

Opening my eyes at sunrise, I was both dazzled and confused by a unique expanse of desert and all it held. Fortunately, for a guide I had Tom Wendt, an experienced desert explorer who was studying botany at the University of Texas. Wendt, photographer Dan Budnik and I had spent the night bedded down among the gypsum flats and dunes on the floor of a small basin called Cuatro Ciénegas, or four marshes, in the Chihuahuan Desert region some 160 miles south-south-east of Big Bend National Park.

On the way here, Tom had told us that the basin, roughly 40 miles square, has no drainage outlet and is thus an example—though atypical —of the land form called a bolson (*pages 136-147*), which is common in the northern Sierra Madre. This particular basin is bisected by the Sierra de San Marcos, a range near the northern end of the Sierra Madre Oriental. We were in the western half of the basin. From my sleeping bag I could look in all directions to distant cordilleras: nearest was the San Marcos, a long, inclined plane backlit by the rising sun.

Beyond my line of vision but very much in my thoughts were the marshes that lay between us and the mountains, receiving their water neither from mountain streams nor direct rainfall. The principal source of water for the marshes—and the source, too, of the gypsum that covers so much of the basin—is a series of thermal springs that rise near the protruding tip of the San Marcos mountains. These springs, aided by an intricate system of subterranean passageways that funnel ground water from beneath the mountains, nourish the special environment of Cuatro Ciénegas. In this meeting place of desiccating desert and oozing wetland exists an astonishing mixture of animal and plant species found nowhere else.

During the November day now dawning we planned to hike from our camp on the basin floor, around the marshes to a small canyon in the Sierra de San Marcos—six miles, perhaps, as the crow flies, considerably farther as we wandered through a variety of habitats. But before we even broke camp, we were rewarded by the sight of a rare yellow flower poking its head above the rim of a neighbouring gypsum dune. Called scientifically *Dyssodia gypsophilia*, it grows only here. It is related to dogweed but has no common name. We dubbed it gypsum dogweed.

Inside the gypsum dogweed lurked a crab spider, a far-ranging, adaptable arachnid. Lying in wait for the pollinating insects they prey on, some crab-spider species can assume the exact hue of a variety of white and yellow flowers. Another ubiquitous desert dweller near our camp was the red-fruited tasajillo,

CRAB SPIDER UPON A DYSSODIA

DESERT CHRISTMAS-CACTUS FRUITS

or desert Christmas cactus. Beware of this plant. Its spines produce a nasty, festering wound. A second common plant growing close by, sprouting among low-lying *Ericameria*, was ocotillo, a long spiny shrub, leafless at the beginning of the dry season. But although ocotillo occurs in other places in the desert, it is only in the Cuatro Ciénegas region that this species appears in intimate association with gypsum.

OCOTILLO AND ERICAMERIA ON GYPSUM FLATS

In the basin of Cuatro Ciénegas the gypsum assumes two guises. It lies in compacted grey flats where weathering of the surface has produced a semi-stable crust, allowing plants and shrubs to take hold. Quite different are the living, moving, dazzling white gypsum dunes that rise 20 to 30 feet above the desert floor. Both forms originate in shallow lakes—such as Laguna Grande about a mile and a half east of our campground—which are part of the system of marshes fed by the warm springs. The spring waters are rich in gypsum and other dissolved minerals. As the water evaporates and the lakes shrink in the dry season, gypsum crystallizes at the margins. The prevailing east wind whips the dry crystals and flakes into billowing dunes, which are slowly and constantly on the move. The grey flats are remnants of dunes long passed.

When we arrived the previous evening, the pristine curves of the dunes had beckoned to us across the flats. Now, come morning, we examined one of the dunes more closely. We looked first at its front wall, arrested momentarily on this windless day in the act of overrunning an area of stabilized gypsum. The ground-hugging plants and grasses at the base of the dune were doomed. Others, like the yucca called Spanish dagger with its spiky green top and shaggy trunk already partly engulfed, might be able to grow fast enough to keep their heads above sand. The mesquite and saltbush higher up had been able to do so.

Animal life was harder to find,

MESQUITE, YUCCA AND SALTBUSH ON TOP OF A GYPSUM DUNE

BLISTER BEETLE ON A MOONPOD STEM

WOLF SPIDER

particularly by day. In the desert the sun is more enemy than friend. Still, its warm hand on our backs was welcome after the chill desert night.

Dan spotted a blister beetle clinging to a moonpod bush. Blister beetles—there are hundreds of species throughout the American Southwest and Mexico—are so called because they produce a toxin that causes a burning rash on contact with human skin. As for the moonpod bush, whose name may derive from its round, greenish-yellow fruit, it is a rare shrub and its presence was one of the treats of our walk in Cuatro Ciénegas. Large portions of the moonpod bush routinely die during drought, but a few green twigs nurture the spark of life.

Two Tiny Predators

We had to dig for two other discoveries. We found a wolf spider some six inches down by opening up its burrow, the mouth of which was a small hole with a delicate half-inch-high lip of gypsum crystals raised around it. Wolf spiders are aggressive hunters, and many species

MACHAERANTHERA AND ANTLION TRACK

ANTLION AMID GYPSUM CRYSTALS

of this family do not spin webs for catching prey. But they do use silk for other purposes—in this case to cement the crystals around the hole and line their burrows. Our specimen, a nocturnal hunter, at first seemed stunned by the light, but soon scurried off under a saltbush.

Even more intriguing than the spider's hole was the odd-looking track we found beside a ropelike plant, endemic to Cuatro Ciénegas, that Tom told us had no popular name but was identified scientifically as *Machaeranthera restiformis*. This strange tracery on the ground grew longer as we watched. The hidden artist, which we dug up a few moments later, turned out to be the larval form of an antlion. Ordinarily antlion larvae dig pits in the sand and wait at the bottom for prey to fall in. This antlion, moving just beneath the surface, may have been looking for a site to dig its pit. While doing so, it left an aimless spoor in the sand, thus living up to its other common name, doodlebug.

After breakfast, around nine, we

GYPSUM CONGEALED AROUND MESQUITE

started hiking eastwards towards the mountains over the crest of the dunes. The high, wispy clouds visible at dawn had evaporated and the sky radiated an intense, almost searing blue. Coming down off the back of the dunes we found ourselves standing in an area studded with haystack-like mounds, some of them about 18 feet high. Tom explained how they had formed: as the wind licked at the back of the dunes, pushing the loose sand forwards, the extensive root systems of the bushes growing on them, mostly mesquite, held on to some of the gypsum.

Not only do the roots form a skeletal structure but, by releasing chemical substances, they seem actually to cement the gypsum crystals into a coherent mass. As the loose material gradually blows past, the mounds remain.

It appears, however, that the mesquite tree is capable of only a temporary holding action. In spite of the roots, the mounds gradually decay, for the nutrients become ex-

hausted and eventually the mesquite dies. The mound then dries out and crumbles away, its remains slowly spreading throughout the area.

Another casualty of the shifting dunes is the Spanish dagger. As we had seen at the front of the dune we examined, this handsome member of the yucca family sometimes grows a long trunk to keep its head above the top of the sand. When the sand blows away, however, the trunk collapses. But the plant often continues to live. We saw several thriving yuccas growing on top of old, gnarled, doubled-over trunks.

On the other hand, a plant like the little red-stemmed gypsum spurge cannot even gain a foothold on the high dunes. Instead, it moves in as the dunes pass, colonizing the flats in low-growing tangles about two feet across.

Finding the Source of the Dunes

Beyond the back of the dunes we crossed a mile or two of largely barren salt flats. Only months ago the *laguna* flooded this plain and even now

SELENITE CRYSTALS

the water table lay just under the surface. But the crumbly residue of gypsum and other minerals left by the retreating lake was too alkaline to permit germination of plant life.

Predominant among the minerals were patches of selenite, the crystalline form of gypsum. These little deposits, about the size of grains of rice, were the basic building blocks of the mighty dunes. Tumbled by the wind, they would be abraded down to particles the size of granulated sugar; and at the same time they would be gathered together until they formed a shifting mass.

After walking for about half an

COLLAPSED YUCCA PLANTS

GYPSUM SPURGE

hour we came to the fringes of Laguna Grande. It had first appeared
as a glassy ribbon shimmering like a
mirage on the basin floor.

On a gypsum mound we came
upon a robber fly feeding on a butterfly. This savage insect descends
like a hawk, seizing its prey—other
flies, bees and wasps—from behind.
Sinking its stout beak into its victim
the robber fly paralyzes it with ven-
om and then sucks out the fluids.

Long before we reached the lake
itself, the ground grew damp. Soon
we were splashing through very
shallow puddles. We took off our
boots and waded the last few hundred yards to the edge of the open
lake. On the way we came upon the
first large and spectacular flowers
we had seen in Cuatro Ciénegas.
This one was a beauty. A marsh
pink, Tom called it, about the size
of a 50-cent piece and common
to coastal wetlands throughout the
American South and into the West
Indies. In central and northern Mexico, however, it grows only in widely
separated inland marshy areas.

A Rare Turtle

We waded into the water, which
seemed cool after our hot walk. Mud
oozed up between our toes. All at
once we spotted a turtle lying on the
lake bottom in a couple of feet of
water. It made no effort to escape as
I waded towards it—strange behaviour for an aquatic turtle, usually
an agile swimmer. And when I
picked it up it simply pulled in its
legs, head and tail and closed shop
by folding its bottom shell up tight
against its carapace. It was a box

LAGUNA GRANDE

ROBBER FLY WITH PREY

MARSH PINK IN FLOWER

BOX TURTLE UNDER WATER

turtle, and a species of the normally land-bound genus *Terrapene*, the star inhabitants of Cuatro Ciénegas.

These small reptiles, known locally as black turtles, grow up to nine inches long, and some years ago their presence triggered a detailed scientific study of Cuatro Ciénegas. Biologically speaking, the basin was not discovered until 1939, when an adventurous American naturalist, E. G. Marsh Jr., began a collection of plants and animals here. The Second World War prevented Marsh's material from receiving the attention it deserved, but from the mid-'40s on, as Marsh's specimens were examined and classified, the list of species unique to Cuatro Ciénegas grew.

The first indication of the significance of the box turtle came in 1958, when John M. Legler and W. L. Minckley—then both graduate students majoring in zoology at the University of Kansas—studied the specimens and discovered traces of algae on the shells. Algae indicated an aquatic habitat. But box turtles of this genus, they both knew, were terrestrial animals. So they rushed down to Cuatro Ciénegas to see for themselves. Sure enough, this box turtle was a swimmer.

Since then, Minckley and his associates have been in the forefront of investigations that have revealed Cuatro Ciénegas as a fascinating biological island where, among other things, the world's only aquatic *Terrapene* is known to exist.

How this anomaly came to be is a matter of some evolutionary disagreement. It was long thought to have evolved from a terrestrial ancestor, adopting aquatic habits in the wet refuge at Cuatro Ciénegas when the surrounding environment became too dry. Current scientific thinking, however, suggests this species of *Terrapene* may be a primitive form that has been aquatic throughout its long evolutionary life in this locale, where conditions on the basin floor have remained relatively stable despite climatic changes. If so, this particular turtle qualifies as a relict that has maintained its original form while other similar species have evolved quite differently. In any case, our aquatic box turtle, like all other turtles, lays its eggs on land and, like all reptiles, breathes air.

MILKWORT BLOSSOMS

We saw several more turtles before we rounded the northern end of the laguna and reached a narrow watercourse. This tributary, according to our map, would be the Río Churince, which we planned to follow to a series of springs called Pozos Bonitos, the river's source. Some river! One hundred yards upstream it was narrow enough to jump across. Yet on closer examina-

SEDGES AND GRASSES BESIDE RÍO CHURINCE

tion, it seemed to carry an impressive amount of water. As it turned out, the Churince was nearly as deep as it was wide, and the banks were sharply undercut—as much as five feet in places. A foot below the surface the river was really twice as wide as it appeared.

I wondered how this had come about, since the current, flowing at about the pace of a slow walk, was hardly sufficient to gouge out the banks. Tom explained that the overhang was not the result of erosion, but rather a combination of plant and mineral growth. Minerals from the rich spring water crystallized like rock candy on the sedges and grasses along the banks. In time, rotted plant material accumulated amid the crystal deposits, and as new plants rooted, the banks grew together. The marsh through which the Río Churince meandered was riddled with streams that had roofed themselves over completely.

There were other surprises in the marsh if one looked closely—for instance, a little plant with a spiky bloom. Tom pointed it out as a succulent polygala, or milkwort. It was the only such milkwort he knew of —and he should know because desert milkworts were the subject of his doctoral thesis. This polygala, as far as anyone is aware, grows only at Cuatro Ciénegas and at similar moist meadows to the south. Close to it we found another plant blooming, a thistle of a type common throughout the American South-west.

Here and there the vegetation was interrupted by small stagnant pud-

THISTLE HEADS

SALT POOL STAINED BY BACTERIA

ALLIGATOR LIZARD

dles with crusted margins. The puddles were mahogany in colour, the shade deepening with the concentration of the brew. I had seen oceanside salt flats exhibiting a similarly ruddy colour, produced by salt-loving bacteria. The same biological factor was at work here.

An Unexpected Lizard

At the edge of one of these miniature clearings Dan spotted a well-camouflaged, six-inch-long brown lizard, its ribs flecked with white. He and Tom agreed that it was a species of alligator lizard. Although they are very fast when striking prey —beetles and small insects—they are relatively slow moving otherwise, and we were able to follow its deliberate steps while Dan clicked away. We did not want to handle it, for when caught by the tail, an alligator lizard is likely to detach that appendage while wriggling free.

Later, when we showed Dan's pictures to a herpetologist, he easily identified the lizard as *Gerrhonotus liocephalus*. That meant we had scored a genuine scoop. The lizard lives throughout much of the Chihuahuan Desert and has even been collected before in the region of Cuatro Ciénegas, but always at higher altitudes. It is an upland lizard, at home in damp forests, and this was the first time our consultant had heard of one being found on a basin floor. The story of how it got there was another matter. Perhaps, like the turtle, it was a relict that had managed to survive.

By noon we were close to the source of the Río Churince. In a few

VEJOVIS COAHUILAE SCORPION

MATING DAMSELFLIES

hours we had walked from Laguna Grande—which I had come to regard as the Mediterranean of this water system—up the Churince to Pozos Bonitos, the enchanting pools from which it rises. I thought of the Nile, and of the years spent discovering its source. Europe, Africa and Cuatro Ciénegas: a far-fetched analogy? Perhaps. But the similarity between this oasis and the Mediterranean—both surrounded by mountains and desert—lingered in my mind.

I was still lost in this reverie when Dan turned up a scorpion under some matted weeds. I wondered immediately whether it was one of Cuatro Ciénegas' 11 endemic scorpi-

on species. It turned out that what we had found was *Vejovis coahuilae*. This fellow, delicate as glass and as belligerent as a bull, is not endemic but instead claims all of the Chihuahan Desert region as its own territory.

Ahead of us a heron flew up—a great blue, judging from its size. We made our approach to the *pozo* stealthily, hoping to see more water birds. In this we were disappointed, yet the pool was vibrant with life. The buzz of insects filled the air. We stopped to watch a pair of damselflies perform their mating ritual on a rapier blade of a bulrush. The iridescent blue male had seized the female by the neck with claspers at the extreme end of his elongated abdomen. Momentarily the female would curve her own abdomen under her partner to touch his sperm duct, completing both the mating act and a perfect geometric figure.

At last we came to the main pool. It was about 30 yards in diameter and 10 to 15 feet deep at the centre, with abrupt banks. And it demanded to be dived into. We had brought a pair of underwater goggles, which we took turns using. What enchantment! It was like swimming in an aquarium. In the centre of the pool, at the bottom, I could actually see water pulsing up through the sediments from underground springs.

An Outpost of Evolution

Hundreds of stubby black-spotted fish, about six inches long, glided about, untroubled by our presence. They belonged to the cichlid family, perchlike freshwater fish common

to Africa and Asia, and occurring in tropical and subtropical waters both there and, less frequently, in the Americas. To my eye they all looked alike, but actually they represented four of the species endemic to Cuatro Ciénegas. Like the box turtles, they were particularly revealing illustrations of the workings of evolution. Taxonomists have discovered that one of these fish has thick, heavy teeth and strong jaw muscles to crush snails. Another, identical externally, has fine teeth and lacks powerful crushing jaws; it feeds on soft bottom debris. Two additional species have more streamlined bodies as well as strong jaws; they prey on other fish.

Isolated for tens of thousands of years, the ancestral cichlid had evolved into four species, each with a different feeding apparatus. Had the waters of the Cuatro Ciénegas basin been filled with more efficient competitors, such diversification might not have occurred.

We were greatly tempted to linger

BULRUSHES AND CAT'S TAILS AT POZOS BONITOS

CICHLIDS NEAR THE POND BOTTOM

GRUSONIA AND LECHUGUILLA ON THE BAJADA

at the *pozo*, but after eating lunch we topped off our canteens—despite its high mineral content this water has no salty taste—and set off towards the San Marcos. The change was as abrupt as if we had set sail from a lush island into a hostile sea. Our ocean was the bajada, the alluvial slope that rises up the front wall of the San Marcos. Its surface is a composite of boulders, gravel and sand. The finer particles have been washed farther away from the mountains, so that the way became increasingly rough.

We had some three miles of bajada to cross to reach the mouth of the canyon that we had chosen as our destination. Cicadas chirruped loudly from the brush; a covey of scaled quail, so named for the look of their plumage, flew up ahead of us. But that was all the animal life we came across. The vegetation was anything but scarce.

Creosote bush is so abundant that Mexicans call it *gobernadora*, or governor, because of its dominance. The English name derives from the heavy, resinous odour of the foliage similar to that of the sticky oils used to preserve wood. After a rainstorm, Tom told us, the air is redolent with it. He liked it, he said. I would as soon sniff a railway sleeper.

Two particular plants imprinted themselves indelibly on our minds. The first was *Grusonia*, a low cactus that grows in thick patches and occurs only in Cuatro Ciénegas and westwards for about 100 miles. Its pulpy segmented body glistens with shiny off-white needles. Everything

LECHUGUILLA FRUIT

LECHUGUILLA FLOWERS

about *Grusonia* says look but keep your distance.

Even more dangerous is lechuguilla, like maguey a member of the large agave family. At first glance a stand of lechuguilla seems to admit passage. But its openings lure the hiker into ever narrower twisting corridors that close in and become traps.

A Thorny Passage

Lechuguilla's weaponry of spines is borne on stiff, leathery leaves that grow from a central core, like lettuce. In fact, lechuguilla means little lettuce in Spanish, perhaps because it was an extremely important food for the early Indians who ate the heart of the plant. Mature plants are typically about a foot high and the margins of the leaves are lined with curved spines. But it is the longer, stouter spines at the ends of the leaves that do the real damage. They readily puncture trousers and even leather, and leave nasty wounds.

Like other agaves, each lechuguilla rosette blooms only once in its lifetime. At the age of between 10 and 25 years—depending on how much moisture the growing plant has received—lechuguilla sends up one spike studded with flowers that vary between shades of red, green and yellow. As these develop into little green fruit, the main rosette dies but a dozen or so shoots spring up around its base. Seeds reside inside the fruit, and if an extended drought kills the shoots, the seeds eventually germinate anyway.

Unlike *Grusonia*, which has no useful purpose, lechuguilla is still harvested, albeit for new purposes.

Its root makes the basis of a good shampoo and fibre from its leaves can be made into twine. For us, however, it proved merely an obstacle to move around.

As we drew closer to the mountain the bajada became steeper. Erosion had eaten deeply into the slope, and we found ourselves climbing up a dry wash with high banks —the entrance to our canyon. Walking in the wash proved easier than on the open flat, however, since here the prickly vegetation had been swept away by flash floods.

At the entrance to the canyon itself we came upon a sotol growing in a cleft in the rock. Wind, funnelling down the arroyo, had whipped its leaves about until they had actually worn a circular pattern into the limestone, a graphic example of the toughness of the plants that

SOTOL ON SCOURED ROCK

survive in such a harsh country.

Inside the narrow canyon, we stepped into shadow and at once were bathed in new sensations. Though there were no seeps or damp spots, on every hand were signs of water. The canyon we had selected is one of the major drainages of the north-west side of the Sierra de San Marcos, and it contains an arroyo that funnels rainwater down the mountainside and on to the bajada. Furthermore, the shaded walls keep water from evaporating as rapidly as it does elsewhere. Wasps, bees, flies and beetles animated the air. Birds called, and there were a few stunted, leafy trees and bushes: acacias, hackberries, desert willows, desert ashes and some small oaks.

At first view the canyon seemed to be a dead end. But as we clambered up the rocks towards a sunwashed scarp, we found that what appeared to be the head of the canyon was merely a right-angle turn. We were in a zigzag fissure that ran deep into the heart of the range between sheer cliffs.

As we came around the turn, all sight of the basin vanished. We were confined, pressed in upon, a strange feeling after the openness of the land behind. It made one dizzy to look up at rocks stacked in impossible piles, ready at the slightest provocation, it seemed, to come crashing down. Some of those that already had fallen were the size of frame houses. The thought of being caught here in a flood was frightening. This was a grinding machine, this canyon and hundreds like it. As these huge boulders were undercut and pushed by flash floods roaring over the canyon floor, they shifted and rolled and ground against each other, loosening fragments that were spewed out on to the bajada.

Now only a brisk breeze came down the canyon. Its welcome coolness reminded us that we had to climb back down and recross the bajada before dark. There would be some light from a threequarters moon, but we did not want to have to pick our way through the *Grusonia* and lechuguilla with flashlights.

We came out of the canyon to the head of the bajada just as the sun was setting. At my shoulder, a blind prickly-pear cactus grew out of the rock wall. The basin lay before us, the dunes where we had slept looked like water in the waning light.

INSIDE THE CANYON

BLIND PRICKLY PEAR GROWING FROM CANYON CREVICE

3/ Where the Birds Are

*There was everything from royal eagles
and many other large birds down to tiny birds
painted in diverse colours.*

BERNAL DÍAZ DEL CASTILLO/ *THE DISCOVERY AND CONQUEST OF MEXICO 1517-1521*

At a village called Gómez Farías the metalled road ended. The drive on the road off the Pan American Highway had been only a short one, but in the village square the cogs of time seemed to have slipped a century or two. I parked in somebody's front yard under mango trees, then transferred my duffle to the back of a waiting truck fitted with facing wooden benches. Overhead a welded iron frame carried a canvas cover, furled now since no rain threatened. All corners and hard surfaces in the truck were padded, a precaution I appreciated as soon as the vehicle lurched out of town and began its whining, grinding, bumping ascent of an ancient logging road. I held tight, but when I arrived at Rancho del Cielo nearly two hours later, I had acquired some bruises.

Sky Ranch, to give the place its English name, nestles at 3,750 feet on the side of a block of the Sierra Madre Oriental called the Sierra de Guatemala. Since 1964 it has served Texas Southmost College, a junior college headquartered in Brownsville, as a field station for the study of the area's flora and fauna. A richer location would be hard to find. The lush valley below is one of the northernmost tropical environments in North America. And surrounding the rancho is a cloud forest, where a unique mingling of tropical and temperate plants supports an amazing array of bird life.

On the late December afternoon when I arrived, a primeval dankness permeated the cloud forest, and a chill was in the air. In the cabin assigned to me, the wood fire crackling in the Franklin stove was welcome. I stood with my back to the warmth while Fred Webster, an avid bird watcher who organizes tours to the rancho, outlined its regimen. Right now, he explained, water was scarce. A gopher had chewed a hole in the line from the main reservoir and before it could be fixed, months of accumulated rain, gathered from cabin eaves, had drained away into the porous limestone substructure of the mountain. A few downpours would alleviate the shortage but until then no showers were allowed. The flush toilets were off bounds, too, so guests would have to use the outhouse—at least during daylight hours. After nightfall the ban on indoor plumbing did not apply. Barbara Warburton, the founder and director of the rancho's field station, did not want anyone meeting a bear or a panther in the dark. Bears and panthers? Yes, Webster told me, I would be surprised at what prowled around in the compound while I slept, and just for good measure he mentioned the jaguar, *el tigre* of the Sierra Madre.

Moments later, as I stowed my gear in a bedroom just big enough for twin double-decked bunks and two chests of drawers, I was brought up short by a rude noise—the *blaat* from an aerosol-powered foghorn. Dinnertime, Webster said; the same *blaat* would signal breakfast.

In the fading light I stumbled up a rocky path to the dining-hall, whose porch commanded a view of a sloping forest glen. Along the path were cultivated plants indigenous to climates farther north: showy azaleas and dwarf peach and pear trees in bloom. In front of the dining-hall was a flat marble tombstone, on which was carved "John William Francis Harrison, Born June 21, 1901, Ontario, Canada—Murdered Rancho del Cielo, Mexico, January 29, 1966." It was Harrison who had planted the flowers and the trees, who had in fact established the rancho and literally given his life for it, as I was to learn.

Six cabins rimmed the compound. Beyond them the forest rose, dark with mystery. But inside, warm and comfortable, we ate dinner by gaslight. The food was basic U.S.A., cooked and served by bright-faced students from Texas Southmost, seeming as out of place on this wild Mexican mountain as were the foghorns and hybrid azaleas. The dinner conversation helped orient me to my surroundings. The eastern wall of the Sierra de Guatemala, on which the rancho perches, is so steep, I was told, that one can stand on a prominence outside the station clearing and look down over the treetops at farmers burning cane in fields in the river valley, more than 3,000 feet below. Above the rancho, the sierra climbs

Under a canopy decked in quetzal feathers, Aztec ruler Moctezuma greets conquistador Cortés in this engraved re-creation of a 1519 scene.

steplike in a series of jagged limestone ridges, which are often wrapped in mist, to a height of 8,000 feet.

The Mountain, as the people at the rancho call their eyrie, lies at the heart of the appealing diversity of habitats that have long made Mexico the breeding and wintering quarters for large numbers of birds. The pre-Columbian peoples worshipped birds, used their feathers for adornment and as articles of trade—and, more mundanely, ate them. The Indians bred, among other species, macaws, parrots and turkeys. The Spanish chronicler Bernal Díaz, who with Cortés and a small band of adventurers entered Mexico City in 1519, was amazed by Moctezuma's aviary, which surpassed any collection of birds known to the Europeans.

In addition to the home-bred birds there were captured ducks and eagles and other bizarre flying creatures that Díaz had never seen before, kept in special boxes where they were meticulously cared for. When Cortés and his men were first presented to Moctezuma, the emperor approached them under "a marvellously rich canopy of green coloured feathers," Díaz reported. The feathers came from the star of the aviary, the quetzal—sometimes called the resplendent trogon. The quetzal's plumes represented valour to the Aztecs, who accordingly embellished their emperors' mantles with them.

Quetzals are the largest of the trogons, a family of tropical woodland birds and the most gorgeously coloured of all American feathered creatures. Their great glory is their tail feathers, that hang down more than twice their body length in a brilliant emerald festoon. Although the Aztecs revered the bird, their lavish use of its feathers for ceremonial occasions reduced its numbers. Even after the destruction of the Aztec nation, the quetzal's beautiful plumage continued to be its downfall: during the 19th Century it was exhaustively hunted to supply the millinery trade of the United States and Europe. And although the quetzal was finally placed on the protected list in 1936, it is now rare in Mexico. One reads that the meek shall inherit the earth—and along with the meek, one is tempted to add, the dull and the drab, since so many of the heroic and handsome creatures like the quetzal and the grizzly bear may well be annihilated by man long before inheriting time.

Fortunately, neither the Aztecs nor later hunters managed significantly to reduce much of the rest of Mexico's avian population—either the native species or the awesome flights of transients. Each winter birds from the north congregate in Mexico—sand-hill cranes, geese, ducks, plovers, sandpipers, gulls, terns, flycatchers, swallows, warblers, finches, buntings, sparrows. One champion northern commuter, the American golden plover, leaves Nova Scotia in autumn and apparently flies nonstop over water to Brazil. On its return trip it loops around and flies home mainly over a land route, stopping off in Mexico.

In all there are some 200 species of these visitors from the north —plus a few birds that fly up to Mexico to escape the South American winters. There are also a few Mexican species that fly south to take advantage of the South American summers. And finally, from time to time, a wholly inexplicable visitor will appear—like the Eurasian émigré, the red-throated pipit. Ordinarily, winter migration takes the pipit to Africa, India, Malaysia or Indonesia.

The migrants join a resident population of some 800 species to make a rough total of just over 1,000. The United States and Canada combined have no more than three-fourths that number, and very few large exotics. Small wonder, considering the greater variety of environments south of the border. Mexico has two seaboards that surpass in length those of the continental United States. There are deserts in the north and rain forests in the south. There are high mountains of all sorts, separated into a multiplicity of ranges, each with its own environment.

The region around Rancho del Cielo contains most of these habitats compressed into an extraordinarily small area. In consequence some 300 species, over a quarter of the count for the entire country, have been seen at one time or another within a few hours' walk of the rancho, making it one of the richest bird-watching stations in North America. And that is why, shortly past Christmas, two Dodge trucks—one of them mine— loaded with expectant bird watchers plus their cameras, tripods, binoculars, telescopes, field guides and rain gear, laboriously ground their way up the Sierra de Guatemala.

The bird watchers, gringos all, were an odd lot. Male and female in equal proportion, they ran the gamut in age from young (from Smith and Princeton) to not-so-young (a grey-haired woman from Texas). Recruited by word of mouth and through advertisements run in publications, they had come to the rancho from all over the United States. There were married couples, singles and married people travelling singly. They had little in common save an insatiable hunger to see birds—to see and to hear them, that is; for let it be known that the term bird watcher is inadequate. To the expert, and these people were almost all experts, audible recognition is half the game. A few of this group of birders —the preferred term among aficionados—had been to the rancho

Resting like living leaves on the jungle floor and random shrubs, these butterflies wear protective tints that match the tree bark and foliage of Sierra de Guatemala's deciduous forest. The group of four different species (top) has left its haven among the plants to feed on sodium salts in a mud patch; a pair of copperhead bollas becomes momentarily unwary during mating; but the calico and the malachite are well camouflaged by the vegetation on which they perch.

A CLORINDE ABOVE OTHER SALT FEEDERS

MATING COPPERHEAD BOLLAS

A CALICO AGAINST MOSSY TREE BARK

A MALACHITE ON A GREEN FROND

before. But most were coming up the mountain for the first time. A group of climbers arriving at Katmandu could hardly have been more alive to the excitement of the moment.

The man who assembled this gathering at the rancho was Webster. A regional editor of the National Audubon Society magazine, *American Birds*, Webster had been visiting the area since 1964. From his first day, he had become enthralled with the great numbers of species to be seen there, and thought, rightly, that others would be too. But that was to be some years away.

The property then belonged to a Canadian émigré named Frank Harrison—he of the marble tombstone outside the dining hall. Harrison, a self-taught botanist, raised tuberous begonias and amaryllises, which thrived in the damp mountain air, and published articles in botanical magazines about the plant life of the cloud forest. He named his homestead Rancho del Cielo. Apart from an occasional trip down the mountain on foot or muleback, Harrison lived quietly with his flowers, his cows and his books.

A handful of ornithologists and botanists, and ordinary Texans who just wanted to get away from it all, were tempted to visit the cloud forest by Harrison's articles. Glad of the stimulating company, he allowed them to camp on his land, and later permitted several of them to build hunting cabins at the rancho, in return for which they paid him a modest annual rent. In 1964, after several groups of Texas Southmost students went there on field trips, the college built its own cabins. Barbara Warburton, who was an early and regular visitor, functioned as director of the field groups.

All this activity captured the attention of some Mexican labourers who were scratching out a meagre existence logging and farming on the mountain. Harrison's farm, they reasoned, must contain a gold mine, judging from the buildings that were rising on it. Why should a single gringo have all that while they and their families were so poor? And so, in profound ignorance, they fell upon Harrison one day in 1966 while he was doing his morning chores and stabbed him in the back. The murderers were quickly apprehended and locked up. Harrison, as it turned out, had deeded his land to a non-profit-making Mexican corporation, with the stipulation that the cloud forest be preserved. Texas Southmost has been the major financial contributor to the rancho, which is administered by the corporation. The Mexican government plans to extend its protection to the rancho by making it a national wildlife reserve.

Six years after the murder, college students under the firm and imaginative guidance of Mrs. Warburton had transformed the rancho from a few cabins in the woods to an operational biological station with a dining-hall, library and dormitories. To help defray expenses, the college had also begun to allow increasing numbers of paying guests to visit the rancho and marvel at its bird life. In 1972, with Webster's enthusiastic help, Mrs. Warburton invited a sizeable contingent of bird watchers to participate in the rancho's first official entry into the Kentucky Derby of bird watching, the Audubon Christmas Bird Count. That year marked the 73rd annual running of the Christmas count and the first time any area south of the Rio Grande had been permitted to enter.

In this intensely competitive—yet intensely good natured—ornithological competition, each year nearly 35,000 bird watchers across the continent fan out 1,300 or so teams to count birds. Each team is restricted to a search area of 15 miles in diameter and to a single calendar day within about a week on either side of Christmas. Any number of bird watchers can participate. The results are collated and published in the April issue of *American Birds*, enabling the various teams to compare their scores. Straight numerical comparisons, of course, have little meaning to many of the purists; the raw number of, say, sea gulls in Boston or swallows in Capistrano is not what your typical Christmas counter tends to care about. For him the pay-off comes in total species recorded —though numbers do have considerable value as preservationist data.

Before 1972, neither Mexico nor any Central American country had been included in the count, for the simple but critical reason that, until then, there had been no heavily illustrated guide to the birds below the border, and hence no sure way to confirm all sightings. But that year two guides came out, each illustrated in colour: Irby Davis' *A Field Guide to the Birds of Mexico and Central America* and Ernest P. Edwards' *A Field Guide to the Birds of Mexico*. With these publications in hand and another one promised, Robert Arbib, editor of *American Birds* and arbiter of rules for the Christmas Bird Count, officially included the lands south of the border in the competition. And he tossed in the West Indies for good measure.

That year the rather hastily recruited bird watchers at Rancho del Cielo came in 12th out of 1,013 reporting areas, and only 34 species behind the winning count of 209 recorded by the winners at Cocoa, Florida. Dazzled by this promising start, Texas Southmost decided to make the rancho a permanent entry. In addition, the college instituted a late-spring bird count. At that season the forest is alive with amorous male birds and the sound of their love songs—seductive, to attract mates, and contentious, to indicate territories and warn other males to stay away.

Thus, bird counting was on its way to becoming an institution at the rancho when I arrived. The big Christmas count was to begin the very next morning, the last day of the year. In addition to the books by Davis and Edwards, I was equipped with another essential publication, *A Field Guide to Mexican Birds,* by the dean of bird-guide author-illustrators, Roger Tory Peterson, and co-author Edward L. Chalif.

After supper and my quick, general orientation to the terrain Webster gathered the troops in the cabin that served as a combined library, laboratory and lecture hall. The experienced bird watchers among the visitors numbered 21. Webster, his wife, Marie, and Mrs. Warburton brought the team total to 24 able-bodied counters. Then there were two hopeless novices—me and my daughter, Heather, who had driven across the country with me—and one dog. The latter, as stated on the papers I had needed to get him across the border at Brownsville, Texas, is a shepherd-beagle mix; he answers, when it suits him, to the name Patrick. Webster, after canvassing personal preferences, divided us into six roving platoons—a pitifully inadequate number, he lamented, to cover the area. But the rancho could accommodate no more. Heather and Patrick were to stay around the compound under the wing of a couple called Anderson who knew the rancho and would make good mentors. The cleared land of the compound itself would be a very productive area for counting. Many songbirds like open spaces or forest edges where flowering plants attract insects for the birds to feed on and where grasses provide additional nourishment in the way of seeds.

I was assigned to Mrs. Warburton's party, the rest of which consisted of Jarvis Beverly, a retired petrochemical engineer from Michigan, and two college students, his protégés on this trip. Charles Munn III, a Princeton student, was something of a bird-watching prodigy. Already, at the age of 19, he had been bird-watching on four continents and had a life list of over 700. That is, he had personally seen more than 700 different species of birds—among enthusiasts roughly the equivalent of a scratch handicap in golf. This was his first visit to Mexico, and I would soon learn how well he had done his homework. Mary McKitrick, from Smith, had recently completed a six-month stint at the Manomet Bird Observatory in Massachusetts. Her special interest was bird behaviour, and she tactfully dismissed the life-list syndrome as being more closely related to stamp and coin collecting than to serious ornithology. None of which diminished her enthusiasm at being in the proximity of so many new birds.

Our party would roam the farthest, using the rancho's two trucks to cross the Sierra de Guatemala to the vicinity of a small, isolated community, La Joya de Salas. On this dry side of the mountain, the birds differ from those of the cloud forest along the way, so in a single day I would see as much variety both in birds and terrain as the sierra offered. We would be climbing out of the cloud forest up to the moist pine-oak forest at 4,200 feet then on to the top of the mountain and down into a little valley of dry pine-oak forest that lay in the rain shadow on the western slope.

Assignments made, Webster concluded the evening by reviewing the check list of the bird species resident in the region. He had already sent a copy of it to each of us, so that we could bone up on our identifications. Mercifully, as it was growing late, Webster hit only the high spots on the list—the difficult identifications, the rare birds.

The next morning, breakfast was served early enough to get the convoy rolling by sunrise. Along the route we dropped three of the other parties, one to be picked up later, the other two to hike back to the rancho. By sometime around 10:30, we had joggled and bumped down a winding canyon and out of the pine-forest into sunlight on a flat, winding valley, backed by yet another wrinkle of the Sierra Madre Oriental. The small village of La Joya de Salas consisted of some two dozen neat stone and adobe houses inside walled gardens. Beyond the settlement, fields of corn stubble and other harvested grains stretched to the visible limit of the valley.

To our left lay a shallow lake. It owed its existence to layers of clay that effectively sealed this limestone sponge and kept the water from percolating away. Perhaps the lake was the *joya*, the jewel, of Salas. Certainly it was its presence that made the little community viable in this arid sector. The water was also the main attraction that had brought us across the mountain; at this time of year, Webster reasoned, the lake was certain to be filled with water birds.

At La Joya we left the trucks and started towards the lake on foot. Right away I had my first field lesson in bird watching. We were strolling through a dry, rocky stretch, sparsely covered with overgrazed grass and acacia. A few small birds flitted through the brush. With an ease and rapidity that was astonishing—even to his fellow bird watchers— Charlie Munn had his tripod-mounted telescope set firmly on the ground and focused on a prospect. "Vermilion flycatcher," he said matter-of-factly, offering me the eyepiece. I recognized the name as one of the minor stars of the Sierra Madre avifauna and for me, a lifer—that is, a species never before seen by the observer. It is not everyone who makes his bird watching debut by logging so colourful a creature.

Sparrow-sized, the vermilion belongs to the family Tyrannidae, or tyrant flycatchers. There are some 65 members of the family in Mexico, and anyone who can recognize them all is a virtuoso. The male vermilion, however, is easy. Among the tyrant flycatchers—including his dowdy mate—he is a dandy, with bright-red underpinnings and crown, black wings, back and tail. Isolated in Charlie's 'scope he was a point of fire. And just as the text in Ernest Edwards' guide predicted, we had found him "in rather arid open country", perched "upright" on a mesquite branch, ready to "fly out to catch insects".

Now Jarvis Beverly had focused his binoculars on another bird. We all turned in unison. No question, we were looking at yet another tyrant flycatcher; the general outline was the same as the vermilion. But the colours were drab—buff on the belly, the rest a dull grey brown. The quandary: was it a male Say's phoebe or a female vermilion? Charlie thought it was a Say's. But the check list that Webster had given us did not include the Say's. It would be a first for the count in this region. Jarvis opted for its being a female vermilion.

While he and Charlie wrangled, I dived into my Edwards. The descriptions of the female vermilion and the Say's phoebe are distressingly alike—so much so that even these experts were at odds on a determination. At that moment Charlie focused on another bird, similar but slightly smaller, perched in the mesquite. This one fitted exactly the description of the female flycatcher, which has a blush of pink on the belly. That made the controversial bird a Say's.

Mary made our next score. Though it was also new to the list, Webster had alerted us to this one. "Keep an eye out for a pyrrhuloxia," he cautioned us, "they like the sort of dry scrub you'll find on the other side of the mountain." And there in dry scrub Mary identified a male pyrrhuloxia. It looked like a faded cardinal to me, even to the crested head. Indeed the two are close relatives, with overlapping ranges. The pyrrhuloxia is found in the South-western United States and across the border as far south as central Mexico, while the brilliant-red male cardinal occurs throughout the Eastern United States, and over most of Mexico. I wondered how Mary had recognized this bird as a male

These birds are among the 197 species that were identified during author Peter Wood's participation in the Audubon Christmas Bird Count in the Gómez Farías region. Each species was spotted in its favoured habitat: the pyrrhuloxia in the arid uplands; the vermilion flycatcher also on dry land but near water; the Altamira oriole in the tropical lowlands; the green jay in the lowlands and the cloud forest; and the blue-hooded euphonia in the cloud forest and wooded uplands.

PYRRHULOXIA

BLUE-HOODED EUPHONIA

VERMILION FLYCATCHER

GREEN JAY

ALTAMIRA ORIOLE

pyrrhuloxia and not a female cardinal. Instead of asking her I leafed through Peterson's guide. It showed the pyrrhuloxia to have a yellow beak, the cardinal a red one, and the body of the female cardinal to be yellow brown, with some reddish tinges on its wings and tail, in contrast to the grey and red of the male pyrrhuloxia. I was learning.

From that fast start the morning wore on interestingly, but without surprises. We spent what was left of it taking a census of water birds, an exercise more dutiful than exciting. Although the primary competition among count areas is the number of different species seen, the more conscientious ornithologists also estimate the number of individual birds seen. By knowing not only what birds are where, but in approximately what numbers at a fixed time each year, preservationists have a bench mark from which to figure migration patterns, to note changing trends and to sound the alarm for endangered species.

The lake was splashed with patches of birds—to my naked eye mere clusters of black dots. Through the 'scope Charlie was able to break them down into coots, grebes, ruddy ducks, shovellers and a half dozen other water birds. While Jarvis filled his notebook, Charlie scanned the lake, singing out, "eight American widgeon, five gadwalls, eight more American widgeon, twenty pintails, four blue-winged teals, thirteen more pintails", and so on, while the rest of us absorbed the sun and watched a small crew of sandpipers comb the muddy edge of the lake.

When Charlie and Jarvis finished, they had noted 13 species. Almost all were migrants from the north, where nature tends to produce prodigious quantities of a single species—in contrast to the tropics where many different species are represented by relatively few individuals. This particular group of ducks, coots and grebes was an infinitesimal fraction of the millions upon millions of water birds that fly south from Canada and the United States each autumn, down the flyways ahead of temperatures that freeze their native lakes, ponds and marshes.

Only a few weeks earlier, 600 miles north-west of the rancho, I had been treated to an early morning view of a typically massive assemblage of such migrants. Some 60 miles south-west of the city of Chihuahua there is a large replica of the little lake at La Joya de Salas. Called Laguna de los Mexicanos, in November and December it fills part of a wide basin with the accumulation of the late summer and autumn rains, then dries up slowly during the ensuing six months of sun. There are hundreds of such transitory lakes and marshes on the interior slopes of the two main ranges, and in the central plateau

Lesser snow geese arrive for the autumn at Laguna de Guzmán in north-west Mexico after a summer of nesting near the Arctic Circle.

Club mosses line the limestone bed of a stream called Indian Springs, flowing through a glade near Rancho del Cielo.

between. The rains that fill them each year seem perfectly timed to welcome birds driven down from the north by snow and ice.

When I saw the Laguna de los Mexicanos, it was some five miles long and three miles across. In all directions the basin rolled away beyond the edge of the *laguna*. Some land was in pasture, some in corn and oats; it was the combination of water and grain that brought the birds each year. Shovellers, pintails and teals splashed and quarrelled among the reeds near shore and in little satellite ponds. Gliding among them like men-o'-war amid scruffy harbour boats, great fleets of snow and white-fronted geese and sand-hill cranes made their regal way.

That day, at sunrise, the light was crystalline, the sky a pale luminous blue, the air icy and still. Mountains circled the horizon, and across the whole wide valley birds were moving and calling. They were just finishing a night spent on the lake. Now they rose from it in squadrons, wheeled together, headed towards the fields and settled like a carpet dropped by the wind. While I crouched behind a hedgerow, a flock of sand-hill cranes, among the wariest of the big birds, landed. This bunch numbered 200 or more, and they passed close enough to spot the ones that were calling in their loud trumpeting voices, close enough to count the individual feathers of their grey wing tips and to feel my neck hairs rise at the sound they made as they ploughed the air.

After they had passed I stood up and scanned the valley through binoculars, watching the movement and counter-movement of the flocks as Napoleon might have surveyed the battle of Austerlitz. There is high emotion in watching so vast a quantity of wildlife on the move. That morning the feeling was intensified—and disturbed—by the knowledge that the guides in Land Rovers who had brought me here had come as anti-preservationist spies. This day was a Thursday. On Saturday, having observed the movements and quantities of birds, our drivers would station weekend hunters where they had stationed me. From the very hedgerow where I crouched, men in camouflaged coveralls would stand up and shatter the morning.

Back at La Joya the morning was melting into the heat of midday. To the east white clouds bulged over the ridge line like a layer of meringue. While we were in full sunshine, the rancho, on the eastern slope of the mountain, was smothered in its customary fog and mist. I thought I had been paying close attention to the birds our own team had been spotting. But at the rancho after supper, when the platoons reported, I was amazed to learn that in the few active hours we were in the field we had spotted 34 different bird species. In all, seven platoons (six at the rancho, one at the mountain's base) reported 197 varieties, a total that would be submitted to *American Birds* as our score.

Much later, in New York, I would learn from a visit to Robert Arbib that the official Gómez area count came in at 10th place. The winner was a Mexican Gulf Coast area called Catemaco, which has rain forest as well as a marine environment. To add to that advantage, Catemaco fielded a team of 52 carefully recruited bird watchers, who staked out the area days before the count was made. The result was spectacular. The Catemaco count fell just eight species short of 300.

By contrast, the bird watchers at Rancho del Cielo, although they focused earnestly on the Christmas Bird Count, were fundamentally a crew of hobbyists who stayed around for five subsequent days in order to revel in the rancho's environment. For me the most interesting of those days was spent walking in a large circle through the cloud forest to the south and south-west of the rancho in the company of a couple named Harms.

Bob Harms, a linguist at the University of Texas, had made only one earlier trip to the rancho, but he knew the local birds remarkably well. He and his Finnish-born wife, Sirpa, a botany expert, made agreeable and informative company for Heather, Patrick and me. With us came the rancho caretaker, introduced by Mrs. Warburton simply as Pablo.

A roadside hawk perched on a stunted tree glares over its shoulder. These small raptors, which never grow to more than 16 inches from head to tail, are named for their habit of perching on fence posts, telegraph poles and wayside trees to scout for their insect, rodent and reptile prey.

At the outer edge of the circle, serving as a destination of sorts, was a place called Indian Springs, about five miles from the rancho. There, a small stream runs out of some rocks sealing a cave in the side of the mountain. We set out along an old logging road that grew narrower and narrower, then petered out in a trail climbing steeply up and to the west. Patrick was constantly disappearing into the undergrowth on either side of the trail. The forest floor was a tumble of limestone boulders and sinkholes. Mrs. Warburton had warned me that although there was no objection to my bringing Patrick, dogs were in some danger in the sierra because of the treacherous topography. He would not be the first dog, she hinted, to disappear, so she suggested keeping him well in hand. That being impossible, I decided to rely on his instincts, however blunted they might be by city life, to keep him out of trouble.

As it turned out, those instincts proved sound. Shortly after we started he flushed a covey of singing quail that flapped off noisily through the trees. Despite their name, the only sound they made was with their wings. Spring and summer—the mating season—are the quails' times to sing. Harms had heard them the last time he was at the rancho, whistling the same notes faster and faster in a furious crescendo. But at any time of year they are timid birds. Without their song to give them away, says one of the bird guides, they are "likely to be overlooked unless accidentally flushed". Score one for dogs.

As we moved deeper into the forest, sun filtered through the canopy. During Bob's previous visit, rain had fallen for the entire six days, he told me, with the exception of a few hours one morning. But the rain itself did not bother him; one came prepared for that. Rather it was the dull, colour-killing light that accompanied it, since colour is the key to the visual identification of birds.

At that moment my eye, casting about in the sun-dappled treetops, caught the red belly and iridescent-green shoulders of a large bird. At last, I thought, a parrot. We all had been looking for parrots, common farther down the mountain, but elusive at the 3,800-foot altitude where we were walking. As a matter of fact, none had been reported by the Rancho del Cielo team on the day of the big count.

"That's no parrot," Bob corrected me. "It's a mountain trogon. Look at its tail." The bird was about the size of an ordinary parrot, but with distinctive tail feathers that jutted down stiffly like the tails of a cutaway coat. Green on the outside, the tail was broadly striped underneath with white and black; in area it was as large as the bird's body. But so well did this bird's tail blend wih the sun and shadow in the top of the large sweet gum that I had completely missed it. Now, as Bob pointed it out, the whole bird popped out at me. And a bit to the left of it on a lower branch I saw its mate.

They were the first large tropical birds I had seen in Mexico. As they sat and watched us out of big, round eyes, I felt I had stepped at last across the threshold of this mountain wilderness. When we moved closer they took off, flying heavily through the treetops. Bob told me these mountain trogons were close relatives of the quetzal.

As we reached the height of the ridge our way led between rocky piles of limestone heaped like gigantic ruins, covered in vines and mosses, the whole sombrely topped by a closed canopy of trees. We passed inviting grottoes and large brush-filled pits formed when the roofs of underground caverns fell in. Suddenly, out of a large depression on our left, a blackish-brown, turkey-sized bird with a bushy crest flew up into a giant maple. Then another went up, and another and another. Crashing after them in hopeless earth-bound pursuit was Patrick.

"Guan," cried Bob and Pablo simultaneously. The crested guan and a related species called the great curassow are among the prime game birds of the sierra forests. The guan can be found on coastal slopes of both the Occidental and Oriental ranges, the curassow mainly on the coastal slopes of the Oriental. Both birds are arboreal, but scratch in the ground for acorns in winter—as these guans had probably been doing when Patrick jumped them. For several days they had been heard around the rancho. Their characteristic cackles and honks had been sufficient identification for them to have been included in the Christmas Bird Count. But until now none of us had seen one. We would probably have walked right by them had Patrick not been working the brush. The guans put on quite a show as they moved through the treetops; and then, before I could really register it all, they were gone.

We stood quite breathless, trying to savour what we had seen. But it had all happened so quickly that it was hard to reconstruct. Someone more accustomed than I to the sight of guans could put it together —someone, for instance, like George Miksch Sutton, an ornithologist and illustrator who had been one of the first bird watchers in the Gómez area. In 1941 Sutton spent several weeks at the base of the mountain and chronicled the experience in a book called *At a Bend in a Mexican River*. There one day he had "watched a pair of crested guans racing nonchalantly forty to sixty feet above ground, leaping from one branch to another without so much as lifting a wing . . . slipping with serpentine effortlessness along the branches, swinging their big tails from side to side to keep their balance". Though they were at times obscured by the foliage, he had never lost "sight of their glowing red throat wattles", a feature I had overlooked entirely. "Finally," says Sutton's text, "flying to a dead tree and running and hopping to the very top, they stood quietly not far apart, as if contemplating the sky." With Patrick barking at them, our guans had spent no time in contemplation.

The curly crested great curassow—which, alas, we did not see—is an odd member of the avian world in that the female is somewhat flashier than the male, her unusual black-and-white-chequered head and throat more distinctive than his yellow-knobbed black head.

My notes list dozens of other birds on the way to the spring and along the long, looping trail we took back. Among them were the acorn woodpecker, so called for its favourite food, which it pounds into holes in a tree, possibly against times of lean feeding; the least pygmy-owl, small and tawny brown with a high-pitched whistle; and the squirrel cuckoo, bright cinnamon with a long tail. Bob Harms called up a number of birds by imitating the trilling whistle of the screech owl. The owl is the natural enemy of all little forest birds—but rather than run from its sound they are attracted to it, possibly to keep the enemy in sight. That night Bob Harms could announce that he had seen three lifers. As for me, most sightings were so brief they blurred in my mind.

One sighting did not. Bob had pointed the bird out to me, high in the top of an old oak, feeding on mistletoe berries. The hour was late and the sun slanted obliquely into the treetop, lighting it like a stage. High up and in clear view was a sole performer, a blue-hooded euphonia —lovely bird, lovely name. Through binoculars that brought it seemingly within reach, we watched for many minutes while the euphonia flitted back and forth, hovering under the hanging berries, plucking one, then darting to a perch to swallow it. The crown and nape of its neck were bright blue, its upper parts a deep, glossy blackish purple. This bird, like the guan and trogon, belongs to the tropical forest. And I felt, somehow, that the sight of it belonged to me.

On our final day, after breakfast, the trucks were scheduled to take all the bird watchers down the mountain again. Rather than submit to the beating I had taken coming up, I consigned my baggage to a truck and set out on foot with the Harmses. We had a head start and it would be an hour or so before the truck caught up with us. A thousand feet down the mountain we saw our first parrots, chattering noisily in the top of a dead tree. As usual, Bob Harms came to my assistance. "Red-lored parrots," he told me. "See the red patch above the beak."

In the village of Gómez two hours later, there was a flurry of good-byes as we separated into our various cars. A mile or two below the village Heather and I spotted a large predatory bird sitting on a fence. I stopped the car and grabbed my binoculars. Suspecting what it was, I told Heather to turn to the appropriate page in Peterson.

While I kept my eye on the bird, Heather read: "Grey brown, rufous barring on underparts." Yes. "Rufous primaries. Tail banded with pale grey and dark brown." Yes. "Habitat—roadsides, woodland borders; mainly lower elevations." Yes, again.

No doubt about it, the bird was a roadside hawk. My first untutored identification—and a lifer, at that.

A Glorious Botanical Confusion

Although the college field station known as Rancho del Cielo near Gómez Farías, Mexico, has recently become renowned as an ornithologist's paradise, it was first established as a preserve for the region's enormous—and anomalous—variety of plants. In fact the same environmental factors that draw the birds have also encouraged the development of a cornucopia of plants.

The rancho benefits broadly from its location on one side of a corridor between Central America and the temperate zone of North America. Here the rancho is in a position to play host to growing things from these two vastly different regions. But although basic geography is one key to the creation of the rancho's plant treasury, the extraordinary variances in local topography and weather exert equal influences. The rancho perches on the eastern flank of the Sierra de Guatemala. a subrange of the Sierra Madre Oriental, 90 miles inland from the Gulf of Mexico. Warm, wet winds sliding in from the Gulf climb the side of the sierra, dumping moisture as they go. At the base of the range, 25 to 60 inches fall per year. In the middle is a moist zone that receives 110 inches. At the top and just beyond the crest, the clouds are spent and plants compete for a sparse 20 inches.

The vegetation varies accordingly; within each zone are natives as well as adaptable immigrants from other climes and lands. At the foot of the mountains is a combination of tropical deciduous forests. In the middle zone, as part of a luxuriant cloud forest, the sweet gum of New England flourishes side by side with the red-berried eugenia of Costa Rica. And over the high ridge line the oaks of a temperate forest are entwined by tropical orchids.

Among the questions botanists are trying to answer is why this unusual combination of species occurred in the first place. One hypothesis holds that advancing glaciers pushed temperate plants southward to the hospitable climate of the Sierra de Guatemala some 25,000 years ago. However, some paleobotanists suggest an earlier date, based on the discovery of fossils of animals that lived in these mountains well before the Ice Age and that normally inhabit regions where temperate vegetation grows. Whatever the facts may be, the Rancho del Cielo region remains an intriguing and beautiful spot where north and south mingle in glorious botanical confusion.

A fan palm (top) and a shagbark hickory (bottom) share the moist forest soil. The fan palm is a rare tropical species exclusive to eastern Mexico; the hickory's normal range is the Eastern United States and Quebec. The fernlike plant between them is a member of the ubiquitous pea family.

A sprig of tropical croton shrub sprouts white male and green female flowers.

Bignonia, a woody climbing vine, reaches maturity in a spray of pink blossoms.

A Forest within a Forest

In the mountains near Rancho del Cielo, the lowest life zone—extending from about 250 feet to 1,800 feet above sea level—contains two different tropical forests.

In one, bombax and acacia trees draped with bromeliads rise out of a dense undergrowth of prickly cactus, croton shrubs and woody vines (*left*). The typical species here are deciduous, losing their leaves in the dry winter season. These same trees are quite common in forests farther south in Mexico and Central America.

Within this dominant forest, much of whose rain water seeps away through its limestone underpinnings, lies a second, quite different forest. This one thrives along the banks of two streams that course through the lowlands, the Río Frío and Río Sabinas (*right*). Here the plants are a fascinating mixture of water-loving figs and cypresses whose relatives range far south, and willows and sycamores whose relatives appear far into the north. Unlike the deciduous trees of the larger forest surrounding them, the moisture seekers either keep their leaves year-round or lose them so briefly that they form a permanent green ribbon along the stream banks.

The broad bases of two Montezuma bald cypresses stand awash in the Río Sabinas during a season of unusually intense rain. Adapted to riverside living and periodic flooding, such trees sometimes survive for over 1,000 years.

A Botanical Kingdom in a Cloud

The lushest vegetation on the east wall of these mountains grows in its moist middle zone 2,200 to 5,500 feet above sea level. At the very centre of this zone lies America's northernmost cloud forest, a 1,500-acre wilderness tract in which both tropical and temperate plants intermingle.

Each year the cloud forest is drenched by six months of rain, beginning in late May and tapering down in late October. During this wet season, the forest is usually veiled in mist. Even in dry months intermittent showers assure enough humidity so that trees, shrubs, mosses, vines and flowers flourish to an awesome degree.

Dahlias shoot up to 15 feet; more than three dozen orchid species thrive (*overleaf*). Though crowded and festooned with epiphytes, the trees—the tallest in the range—grow to 100 feet. Four sugar-maple species occur here—twice the number found in the New England woods with which they are commonly linked.

But the greatest wonder of the cloud forest is its even-handed hospitality. Living side by side are maple and *Podocarpus*, sweet gum and *Cedrela*, hickory and palm, and a host of other plants that more often grow thousands of miles apart.

Blurred by a low-hanging haze, oaks and sweet gums rise out of the cloud-forest undergrowth. The shrubs in the foreground—all natives—are, from left, a Humboldt butterfly bush, a poisonous mala mujer and a scarlet runner bean.

SERPENT HEAD